Killer

Success Strategies for Young Professionals

By Frederick W. Ball and Barbara B. Ball

The sponsoring editor and the editing supervisor for this book was Armi Karell Roxas.

Ball & Associates, LLC

First published by Dog Ear Publishing
4010 W. 86th Street, Ste H
Indianapolis, IN 46268
www.dogearpublishing.net

ISBN: 978-160844-348-2

Ball, Frederick W.
        Killer Interviews: Success Strategies for Young Professionals / Frederick W. Ball,
Barbara B. Ball.
Includes index.
1. Employment preparation, networking and interviewing.

This book is printed on acid-free paper.

Printed in the United States of America

www.thekillerinterviewsolution.com

thekillerinterviewsolution@comcast.net

To Jay, Erica, Katherine, and Mike who have provided invaluable strategic, tactical, and marketing advice, and, even more important, continuous support and love.

Table of Contents

www.thekillerinterviewsolution.com

PART I

Transitions

The transition, from school to job or job to job, requires a well prepared and executed game plan.

- Transitions of any kind cause stress.
- There is a good deal of effort to land a great job in a highly competitive job market.
- The keys are:
  - **PREPARATION**
  - **PRESENCE**
  - **PRESENTATION**
  - **PASSION.**

Change Presents Great Opportunity

Jason approached his upcoming interview with the same sense of excitement and adventure as everything else in life. And why not? He had always been successful. He ranked third in his high school graduating class, was president of the student government, and was captain of the lacrosse team. His SAT scores were 1370. He had been accepted at three prestigious schools and selected Cornell.

Early in his first year, he thought about financial services as a possible career path. In his sophomore year, he declared economics as his major. Jason knew he would have to maintain a highly competitive grade point average if he were to realize his dream. By working hard, he maintained a steady 3.5 GPA.

In addition to the academic requirements, Jason also needed two sought-after internships in financial services. Sophomore year, he went through the interviewing process, which seemed pretty straightforward, focused on his skills to perform successfully and was offered an internship. Junior year interviews were more intense, particularly because he knew there was the possibility of a forthcoming job offer at the end of the summer.

He found the interviews challenging, yet fun, and landed an internship at JP Morgan Chase (sophomore year) and another at a well-known hedge fund (junior year.) Jason discovered he actually enjoyed the smaller company more, but the hedge fund was not in a position to offer him a job at the conclusion of summer due to a downturn in their business.

He returned for the start of his senior year energized and ready to go with two goals: continuing to do well in his courses, and landing an exciting job. Yet, he also knew he had been successful with a fair, but not burdensome amount of effort, and expected the same in the interview process. He developed a resume and practiced some general interview questions a friend had downloaded from the Internet. Everything seemed set. He truly felt he would be an excellent candidate because he was physically and mentally prepared, his GPA was high and his internships had been excellent. He landed interviews with a number of companies.

Within the first few minutes of his initial interview Jason knew he was in deep trouble, and, by the time he arrived home, he was in shock. So many things went through Jason's head. He had been fortunate since so much of his success had come easily. Now he was facing the real world and he had encountered a savvy, intelligent, perceptive interviewer from an A+ company. He knew he had failed the test, and, when he did not get called back, it came as no surprise.

After a few days of feeling sorry for himself and dealing with a serious case of self-doubt, he knew he needed to reassess his interview game plan. He was lucky to be able to schedule a meeting with one of his professors who consulted to top companies. The professor asked Jason for a quick review of what happened. The question that immediately came to his mind was when the interviewer asked, "What makes you unique?"

Jason said he was able to discuss a few of his skill sets such as his drive and his willingness to remain focused until the job was done. The professor nodded and Jason went on, "Then she (the interviewer) asked for a specific example that illustrated my drive or perseverance and when I gave that to her, she probed deeper into the accomplishment, by asking about what obstacles I faced, and what I had learned."

"Go on," responded the professor.

"That's it," said Jason. "I didn't have the details at the tip of my tongue and I bumbled my way through those questions and the rest of the interview. She dug down into each of the responses I gave for every question. It was as if I were at an inquisition."

The professor smiled. "Excellent interviewer; she was getting at who you are and how you think."

Jason was amazed. "But no other interviewer has done that."

"That's not surprising," said the professor. "There aren't a lot of excellent, or even good, interviewers. But now you've learned if you want to compete for the best jobs you have to be ready to interview with outstanding interviewers."

"There's no way I want anything less than the best job; so, will you help me? What do I need to do?"

The professor was a little taken aback, yet amused, by Jason's boldness. "I'm tied up in consulting projects right now, but I can give you an executive summary. After that, you'll need to do the work to put meat on the bones."

The professor was explicit as he gave Jason an overview of the hiring process, indicating that a step-by-step strategic game plan for winning the best job requires:

- Preparation- establishing an organized game plan of resume building, networking, and interviewing successfully.
- Presence-the self-confidence to build a partnership with the interviewer.
- Presentation/Execution-the ability to execute your game plan during the interview and to "close the sale."
- Passion- the fire and relentless drive to initiate, execute, and achieve results.

"Although I've mentioned all four P's, my focus centers on Preparation," said the professor. "Preparation, as you've discovered, is often a major stumbling block for young professionals because they simply don't prepare enough. You need to prepare your answers in the areas where the interviewer is most likely to concentrate:

- Threshold competencies-do you demonstrate intellect, problem solving, and technical skills? You will be asked for details of your academic training, extracurricular activities, internships, and positions you've held.
- Character-do you demonstrate maturity in decisions dealing with people and personal choices? You will be asked to present accomplishments, including details, and you will be evaluated on the quality of the accomplishment and the manner in which you behaved, especially as you dealt with people.
- Fit-do you demonstrate the relationship skills to be a strong team player and to exhibit leadership when called upon? You will be evaluated on your ability to build rapport with the interviewer, your behavior in the interview, and the interviewer's assessment of how you will relate to her company's people.
- Job competence-do you demonstrate the potential or experience to perform successfully? The interviewer will be interested in your projects, activities, internships, or work experience, and how they demonstrate your ability to perform.
- Results orientation-do you demonstrate a deep concern for producing sustained results in everything you do? The interviewer will evaluate whether you volunteer the bottom line results for each accomplishment you give her and whether you are really excited about achieving those results."

"Just one last thing," said the professor. "Passion is the tie breaker. The interviewer looks for someone who wants the job and will bring desire, motivation, energy, and relentless drive. It includes the optimism and enthusiasm to be a self-starter, the ability to energize others, and to set and meet goals. You will be asked why you are excited about working for the company and industry. You may be asked about one of your passions, including the details. If you do what I've suggested, you'll be in great shape."

Jason took the professor's words to heart. He worked hard to prepare thoroughly, and ultimately landed an excellent position, learning an important lesson in the process. The best firms understand how much effort is involved in hiring the outstanding candidate, and they are committed to do what it takes to be successful. This means involving a number of highly paid executives, and taking valuable hours away from direct production for the firm. Great hiring, however, will make their company more competitive and increase production in the future. Any interviewer from an A company will tell you the differences among the best candidates are often extremely small, and a candidate's thorough **Preparation** is critical. **Presence, Presentation** and **Passion,** which are equally important, will be discussed throughout the book.

Summary

In order to win the best possible job you will need:
- Preparation: establishing an organized game plan, which includes resume building, networking and interviewing successfully.
- Presence: the self-confidence to build a partnership with the interviewer.
- Presentation/Execution: the ability to execute your game plan during the interview and to "close the sale."
- Passion: the fire and relentless drive to initiate execute and achieve results.

Preparation for the job interview requires attention to those areas where the interviewer is likely to focus:
- Threshold competencies-intellect, problem solving, and technical skills.
- Character-maturity in decisions dealing with people and personal choices.
- Fit-relationship skills that evidence a strong team player with leadership ability when called upon.

- Job competence-the potential or experience to perform success-fully.
- Results orientation-relentless drive to produce sustained results.
- Passion-love of life and work, optimism, and enthusiasm, with the ability to energize others.

The quality of your answers will be one of the keys to your success.

Competition and the Need for a Plan

This book coaches you on how to prepare for, land, and achieve success in the "killer interview" for the job you really want in business, education, not-for-profit, or government service. It is for college students, recent college undergraduates, graduate students, and young professionals who may be interested in a job or career change.

As you read in the previous case study, Jason's original strategy for the job interview enabled him to participate, but not to win. His strategy was based on dealing with an average interviewer in a far less competitive job market, and when he encountered an excellent interviewer, he failed.

Our goal is to prepare you to win an outstanding job. We have divided the book into six sections, one for each phase of the job campaign.

Part I: Transitions sets the stage with a case study focusing on competitiveness in the marketplace, the need to have a strategy if you are to be successful, and the strength of your will to win.

Part II: Preparation defines what is needed before you enter the competition. Psychological, physical, and intellectual preparation takes time, thought, and determination. It is easy to rationalize:

- I am a confident person, and that will show in an interview (regardless of my degree of preparation.)
- I am a high-energy person (despite being unfit physically and unable to remain focused by the third consecutive interview.)
- I am able to discuss any facet of my skills and abilities in detail (despite my inability to cut to the heart of the matter by citing specific competencies and defending them with appropriate bottom-line accomplishments.)

Preparation also includes creating a powerful, congruent résumé which presents your strengths and bottom-line achievements. Reviewing your résumé just before meeting the interviewer is a great way to be ready to present yourself with assurance.

Part III: The Power of Networking provides a discussion of how a network sales force can help you land exciting interviews. The open job market, posting on the Internet, newspapers, employment agencies/search firms and company websites, are far easier to use and require less effort, but the yield is far lower than networking. Networking is tapping into the hidden world of referral where you may be the only candidate and you may be interviewing with a friend, or a friend of a friend. Networking requires a system and simple analysis to be sure you are providing the necessary follow-up.

Part IV: Presence is having the self-confidence to build a partnership with the interviewer. Self-confidence comes with understanding the parts of the interview, and how the interviewer and you will approach the interview. In this section, we discuss the content interview from the interviewer's perspective and from your perspective to prepare you for what you will face. We then discuss final preparation for the interview.

Part V: Presentation and Passion: Successful Interview Behavior deals with interview sequence and successful interview behavior. Interview sequence provides you with the confidence to know what will happen in the interview and when. Transition from one phase of an interview to another is important knowledge to assist you to stay in step with the interviewer.

Human interaction and communication are the elements that make an interview come to life. Your goal is to engage in a stimulating, exciting, interactive conversation with the interviewer. To accomplish this, you need to be aware of the communication patterns that will likely dominate various phases of the interview in order to determine how you can impact the discussion in a positive manner.

It is important that you evaluate your behavior during the interview so you can make subtle adjustments to become the successful candidate. A more detailed evaluation follows the interview when you can make any needed adjustments for the next interview. Finally, you will need to accomplish some tasks after the interview to make sure your candidacy stays on track.

Part VI: Selecting the Company is a guide to help you select the right company. While the company is determining whether *you* are the best fit for the position, you should be doing your own investigation to decide whether *this* is the best position and company for you and your career. Due to its importance, the buy side investigation (this is where you become the buyer) should begin when the company expresses interest in you and run concurrently with the sell side activities (when you are selling your abilities.)

In addition to selecting the right company, you want to be prepared to negotiate the best, and most fair, compensation package. We give you the tools to do that.

PART II

Preparation

Establishing an organized game plan to prepare for resume building, networking, and interviewing successfully.

- Psychological: overwhelmingly positive attitude and self-confidence.
- Physical: ability to remain focused and sustain high energy during multiple interviews on the same day.
- Intellectual: knowledge of competencies, accomplishments, and uniqueness.
- Resume: preparation of your primary marketing document.
- Company research: the necessary due diligence to learn about the company.

Step 1: The Mind Game

Recently, we overheard a conversation in the subway between Caroline, a new college graduate, and Josh, a young professional with five years' experience. Caroline was on her way to a job interview for a position she really wanted in the publishing business. It was clear from her comments that she had done all the right things up to this point. She had an excellent background, prepared well, and networked her way effectively into this interview. Yet, she was visibly nervous.

Josh felt sure his interviewing strategies were outstanding. He stressed being fully prepared for questions about education and summer internships. Caroline said she was and proved it by being able to answer the questions he asked her.

After hearing her responses, he pronounced, "Terrific, you really are prepared. The key to your interview is your ability to react quickly and show your preparation by giving fast responses to the interviewer's questions. Most important, never let them see you sweat!"

Josh's remarks were encouraging, but way off the mark. Thorough knowledge of your education, work history, and being quick on your feet all help to be considered for a position, but this sounded like a job Caroline really wanted—the kind that doesn't comes along too often. This was the killer interview, and she would have to do a lot more than follow the advice she had heard.

The case for preparation is overwhelming. If you're an athlete, actor, debater, musician, you know the importance of preparation. Prepare, prepare, prepare is to interviewing what location, location, location is to real estate.

Unfortunately, preparation is often seen, not in the larger context of being an integral part of interview planning, but as a specific, last minute act to cram in a few facts. You'll sometimes hear, "I don't need much preparation. I'm extremely agile in an interview." This is a formula for a candidate to be turned down for an excellent opportunity, only to discover later that he was perceived as arrogant, shallow, or ill-prepared. Psychological, physical, and intellectual preparation needs to be launched on the same day as the decision to seek employment or change positions.

When preparation is undertaken early in the job campaign, every aspect of the interview process can be addressed. Spending time thinking about an interview gives you an opportunity to develop and fine-tune your approach to various issues. An interview consists of exchanging thousands of words with every interviewer you meet. So, the choice between two very competitive candidates often swings on abbreviated exchanges of a few words each.

Fears Associated with Change

There is clearly a win/lose aspect to a job campaign that causes emotional highs and lows. Self-confidence can be high at one moment, and low at another. This happens to every person who has ever entered the job market, regardless of level or function or personal circumstances. During low points, fears and questions creep into your mind. Fears fit into a number of general categories, and, once they are understood, it is possible to understand how your inner strength will overcome them.

Lack of Self-confidence

Your view of self is so closely tied to job success that, if you are looking for your first job, are between jobs, or are unhappy in your present job, your self-concept is affected. Whatever the reason, the effect can be the same.

Questions:
- Am I prepared for the rigors of interviewing?
- Will I maintain my sense of purpose?
- Will I maintain my self-respect?
- Will the new people I meet while networking or interviewing like me?

Negative Reactions

A concern is that family, friends, classmates, or business associates will react negatively if you choose a career direction other than what they might choose for you. In the same way that self-concept is often measured by school or job success, the reaction of others is another way people measure how they are doing.

Questions:
- Will my family support me through this process?
- Will they understand that getting a job offer takes time?

- Do they understand I need the right job for me, not a job for others?
- Will my friends be too busy for me at a time when I need them?

The Unknown

This fear surfaces whenever someone enters the job market or re-enters after an absence. If you are entering for the first time, you normally feel apprehensive about facing a new or different challenge. If you are entering the job market after being away from it, your concerns are with current market conditions and your marketability.

Questions:
- Am I marketable?
- Am I too young, inexperienced, or generalized?
- How do I approach a job interview in this climate?
- Is the job market more difficult now than when I last searched for a job?
- Will I be able to secure a position fast?

Positive Characteristics

If these fears could not be overcome, this would be a depressing chapter. Fortunately, that's not the case. Preparation, along with knowledge of inter-viewing skills and strategies, builds self-confidence—*and that self-confidence snowballs.*

When you have your first good interview, you build additional confidence. You begin to realize the skills and abilities you developed (which often go unnoticed in the routine of daily life) have moved you to a higher ability level. When an interviewer expresses interest in you (whether you receive an offer or not,) it makes you stronger for the next round of interviews. A set of inner strengths and characteristics begins to take over.

Overwhelmingly Positive Attitude

It is generally held that people who have positive attitudes can truthfully say:
- I believe in myself.
- I am capable of anything I set my mind to.
- I use my thoughts, emotions, actions, and time wisely.
- I give myself time to reflect.

All of us would love to be highly positive 100 percent of the time. But, since we are human, we have some ups and downs. On down days, it's helpful to have a positive role model.

Your role model could be anybody. It could be a parent, a teacher, a coach, or perhaps a sibling or friend. It needs to be someone who taught you to believe in yourself to the point where you didn't think you could lose.

It is a given that most people would rather work with a "positive, can-do, let's make it happen" person. Job candidates know the importance of being positive. Despite their best intentions, however, many candidates, if given enough time, tend to volunteer negatives or perceived negatives about themselves. This happens at all levels, from recent graduates through executives.

When asked why he selected the college he attended, a candidate might respond, "I selected college X because I wasn't as good a student as my sister." Did anyone ask about your sister? No. But the person's perception was that there was a weakness regarding the college he/she selected. The issue might never have entered the interviewer's mind, but now it is a potential negative thrown on the table by the job applicant himself.

Why does this happen? It is probably because many of us have been brought up with the notion that humility is a virtue, and, in an effort to give "full disclosure," we volunteer negatives. We have no quarrel with honesty—it is absolutely essential. But an interview is not the place to be self-effacing, especially if you are not even asked to comment on the topic.

Interview Tip! Positive Thoughts and Behavior
You simply cannot allow negative thoughts or comments to infiltrate your presentation. You must be consistently positive in selling your strongest skills and abilities.

Total Commitment to the Task

Commitment requires that:
- You understand your goals.
- You believe the task is consistent with your values.
- You accept what needs to be accomplished.
- You have the spirit and the will to succeed.

What degree of commitment is necessary to land a new position? You need a lot more than most people think. Once you have identified a position, commitment and enthusiasm are critical to your success in the interview. Any good interviewer is looking for signs that indicate an interest and enthusiasm for the work.

Commitment is almost always visible to a knowledgeable interviewer. So is a lack of commitment. The signals will be broadcast through the course of an interview (not always consciously.) The knowledgeable and experienced interviewer will pick them up.

An Intelligent, Organized Game Plan

A game plan can be divided into logical objectives:
- You will identify what needs to be done.
- You will schedule time wisely.
- You will manage time to meet deadlines.
- You will evaluate results and make changes as necessary.

Organization is a critical ingredient to success. As you begin your job campaign, physical preparation will be as important as intellectual preparation. Intellectual preparation requires organization to identify your major skill sets and to determine the accomplishments that best illustrate your skills.

You also need to be organized as you identify the target companies you plan to pursue. Once you are invited to an interview, you need to research the position, the company, the products and/or services, and the people. This may require seeking information from the company, identifying and speaking with people who know about the company, using the Internet or library research, or any other means of obtaining information. At the conclusion of your first round of interviews, it takes discipline and organization to send thank you letters (or emails) promptly.

When you're called for a second round of interviews, you'll need to learn as much as possible about the people interviewing you (both personally and professionally.) If possible, gather additional information about the company so that you'll be able to participate in a knowledgeable business conversation during the interview.

After the interview, continue your due diligence, checking with individuals who know about the company, such as suppliers or customers, employees, consultants, bankers, lawyers, or accountants. The more thorough your knowledge gathering, the less chance for surprises and the greater chance for success.

Perseverance and Determination

The personal actions associated with perseverance and determination are:
- I will act now.
- I will stretch myself.
- I will learn from my experiences and mistakes.
- I won't quit until I succeed.

Of these characteristics, we are convinced that "I will act now" and "I won't quit until I succeed" matter most. In a job campaign, just as with any other challenge in life, there will be peaks and valleys. Fred's dad kept a quotation attributed to Calvin Coolidge for years that got him through some rough times:

> Nothing can take the place of persistence in the world. Talent will not; nothing is more common than unsuccessful men with talent. Genius will not; unrewarded genius is almost a proverb. Education alone will not; the world is full of educated failures. Persistence and determination alone are omnipotent.

It's stories of people dealing with adversity that make abstract concepts like perseverance and determination hit home. We believe in the power of role models or heroes as inspiration to help us rise to a challenge and be successful.

When students in various urban schools were asked for their heroes, they named sports giants like Tiger Woods or Payton Manning, and celebrities like Oprah Winfrey. When asked why heroes matter, their answers were simple: "They work hours and weeks and years until they are the best. They overcome adversity. They never give up." What these students seem to be saying is heroes are proof that any task can be accomplished if there is a strong enough belief and desire to accomplish the goal.

Impenetrable Self-Confidence with Humility

The aspects of impenetrable self-confidence are:
- I will succeed because I have prepared extremely well.
- I will succeed because I have an outstanding game plan.
- I will succeed because I believe I will succeed.

Impenetrable self-confidence is the degree to which you believe in yourself. Entering the job market can be scary. On one hand, your life successes give you strength and confidence. On the other hand, there may be
a self-appointed, "helpful" critic behind every door who wants to look at
your career plan and make suggestions. Too often, they are negative or
incorrect.

You combat this with impenetrable self-confidence. Once you have done
your homework and selected a realistic, attainable target, move ahead.
Don't let anyone discourage you from reaching the goal. Push on. Success
will follow.

Summary
The internal strengths you can summon during your job campaign are:
- Overwhelmingly positive attitude.
- Total commitment to the task.
- Intelligent, organized game plan.
- Perseverance and determination.
- Impenetrable self-confidence.

Taken together, these extremely powerful strengths can be used to overcome any fears or concerns that surface. The bottom line is simple. If you
have an overwhelmingly positive attitude, are committed to a realistic and
worthwhile goal, and if you pursue it with organization, perseverance,
determination, and impenetrable self-confidence, then you will be successful.

Step 2: Become Physically Fit

Physical exercise is not often mentioned in connection with preparation for a job campaign and interviewing. It should be. If you're fit, then you will feel better about yourself, you'll be "on your game" with high energy and resilience, and you will perform better. You will also demonstrate an overwhelmingly positive attitude and impenetrable self-confidence.

Your fitness will be on display when you walk into the interview because the first thing an interviewer observes--before a word is spoken, before anything else happens--is fitness and energy. It is the first value judgment. Fitness creates a perception of self-confidence, energy, and drive.

Do these thoughts actually occur to interviewers? Absolutely. Do they affect the decision making process? Yes. Are they fair? Immaterial. Physical fitness is part of an important first impression.

Career Profile
Energy Reserve

Evangelia was an extremely popular member of her college graduating class. She had outstanding interpersonal skills; people were drawn to her immediately. In addition, she was an outstanding student, and her scientific background put her in a very advantageous position as she began to focus on life after college and a job. Then, seemingly out of nowhere, Rob, her boyfriend since freshman year of college, announced he needed some space and wanted to date other women. It was a devastating blow. She was depressed and quickly became tough to live with. The next few months were very difficult as she began to come to terms about life without Rob.

Finally, Evangelia felt the healing process begin to take place. Partly due to the healing process and partly due to the necessity of finding work, she started to focus on finding a position. However, her energy reserve still wasn't there. Some days she felt high energy, and other days she found it difficult to get out of bed. Her friends intervened and talked her into joining their yoga class.

Evangelia was astonished by the direct correlation between her increased energy and the return of her self-confidence. She then bought a great new suit for interviewing; she knew she looked her best and felt great. She made a positive initial impression when meeting the succession of interviewers, and she landed the job she wanted after a series of intense interviews.

Mental Alertness

Initial impression is reason enough to place importance on fitness. However, what happens over the course of the entire interviewing process is also extremely important. Is interviewing physically exhausting? Ask anyone who has interviewed recently. The answer is a resounding, "Yes!" Now suppose that, instead of one interview, there are two, three, four, or more interviews on the same day.

The need to be physically prepared for the possibility of multiple interviews in one day is critical—and is definitely a trend that is on the rise. No doubt, some firms feel energy and drive are critical elements in the success quotient for a position. One means for them to test these characteristics is to schedule multiple interviews deliberately on the same day. More often than not, however, in this era of "lean and mean" operations, scheduling multiple interviews is a necessity when the interviewing executives are in town or can break loose from other meetings. Multiple interviews are exhausting and require excellent physical conditioning, as well as mental preparation.

Along with outstanding fitness, mental alertness is another important result of a fitness program. Physical conditioning and mental alertness go hand in hand. You must be as physically prepared and as mentally alert at the end of your last interview (perhaps five o'clock on a Friday afternoon) as you were at the beginning of your first interview. Mental alertness provides the self-confidence and stamina required to remain positive and focused through one or more interviews.

Fitness

To achieve physical conditioning, then, the best systems are aerobic exercise programs, and the best exercises are swimming, bicycling, walking, and/or jogging. This is not a haphazard once-in-awhile program, but a systematic three to six times a week regimen. As with any plan, it is important to build up slowly until you reach full strength. Exercise more times per week, rather than less. The schedule should start on the first day you decide to seek a job, or job change, and it should continue throughout your campaign. (Note: any exercise program should be conducted under the direction of your doctor.)

Your routine helps you be in outstanding physical shape when you are called for interviews. Working out on the day of the interview can assist you to relax and remain focused. How much should you exercise on that day? You should do no more than you have been doing in your regular program. A good rule of thumb is to do no more than 65-75 percent of a normal workout. You want to do enough to relax, but not so much that you're tired. With the appropriate amount of exercise, your head is clearer, and you keep the interview in perspective.

The concept of physical activity before something important is not new. In acting, for example, it is commonplace. A new female lead had been hired for a highly successful Broadway play, and it was her first night. She was so nervous she was almost ill, and was afraid she wouldn't be able to perform. Instinctively, she began to walk. She found herself in the deep shadows behind the stage. As her eyes adjusted to the dark she thought she saw a person in the corner. It was the star of the show. Hands pressed against the wall, he was doing exercises. He stopped when he saw her, and realizing how upset she was, he insisted that she join him. No one said "no" to the star, so she nervously joined him. Soon the physical exercise relaxed her to the point that she could begin her normal breathing exercises. Her first performance on stage was outstanding.

Finding time to exercise on an interview day offers other potential benefits, such as allowing you to forget the pressures of your present job or activities, and helping you to focus on various aspects of the upcoming interview. Exercise on the day of an interview pays significant benefits.

Career Profile
Arriving Early

Charlie had an interview for an entry-level analyst position at a consumer products company about 150 miles from campus. Since the interview was at 9:30, he decided he would leave campus early, and drive the three hours in the morning to avoid the expense of a hotel. A few days before the interview, he mentioned his plan to one of his professors.

"Oh, no you won't," the professor said. "This interview will decide your fate with the company, and you need to be early and well rested. You need to get there the night before and get a good night sleep." Charlie was surprised by the professor's comments, but decided to follow the professor's advice.

Charlie was glad he decided to arrive early because the company was built in a campus type organization and it wasn't easy to find the right building. When he arrived at the designated location, it was about 20 minutes before his interview. He met Ms. Lopez's administrative assistant, who was very pleasant. She clearly knew the candidates were all seniors in college and did everything she could to make Charlie comfortable. During their initial conversation, Charlie discovered they had grown up not far apart, and knew a lot of the same people. He suddenly felt as if he had an ally. He felt a great deal more relaxed when it was time for his interview and he felt he did well with Ms. Lopez.

When he got back to campus, he made a special trip to see the professor whose advice he had taken. He thanked the professor and told him how wise the advice had been. A few weeks later, Charles was offered a job.

Summary

An exercise program (walking, swimming, bicycling, and/or jogging) should be undertaken at the beginning of a job search (under the direction of your doctor) and implemented three to six times per week. The benefits include:
- Fitness.
- Sufficient conditioning to withstand the rigors of interviewing.
- Increase in energy and stamina.
- Relaxation and stress reduction.

Step 3: Assess Your Competencies and Accomplishments

Preparation, presence, presentation, and passion are equally important in winning a great job. Initial preparation for the content portion of the job interview is the subject of this chapter and will be followed by building a résumé and gathering data about the company. Presence, presentation and passion will come later in the book. **Content preparation ensures complete knowledge of your competencies, major skill sets, accomplishments, and success stories that demonstrate how you have effectively used the competency in a real life situation.**

Preparation is an enigma. On one hand, job seekers acknowledge the importance of preparation. On the other hand, many of them spend a minimal amount of time analyzing their competencies and accomplishments, saying that it's unnecessary because they know themselves and don't need to spend much time in preparation. This is the old "pay me now or pay me later" dilemma. Time spent in preparation clearly pays dividends in the job interview, and cuts the time to landing a new position. And, just as important, preparation dramatically increases the probability that it will be the right job.

If lucky, the unprepared job seeker meets a knowledgeable, professional interviewer early in his job campaign who shatters the idea that knowing yourself intuitively is synonymous with preparation. (That was the case with Jason whose case study we discussed earlier.) We say "lucky" because it is better to learn the lesson quickly, and not lose a lot of time. The tough questions come with specific focus that demand direct answers. For example, the interviewer might ask, "What are your three or four critical abilities that will help you be successful here?" What's really being asked couldn't be clearer! "Why should I hire you? What skills will you bring to my organization?" Some people say that a question like that isn't so tough. They rattle on about, "New business generation…my ability to deal with people…my marketing and research background…solving problems." Wrong answer.

Three to Four Key Competencies (AKA skill sets)

What's wrong with that answer? It just isn't that easy. You must be sure the three to four competencies you highlight are your best abilities. There is no second chance. You probably have a great number of competencies, but that isn't what you were asked. You were asked to select your *best* competencies for this organization. Think of the presentation of your competencies as focusing the interviewer on the skill sets you could bring to the organization.

Since the interviewer is a busy person who hasn't been thinking much about you before you arrive, it is helpful for the interviewer to understand your competencies. One further point—do not be concerned that other candidates might have some or all of the same competencies you do, especially when you are just starting out. It is your accomplishments that will separate you from the rest.

Interview Tip! Three to Four Competencies

Present your three to four best competencies to assist the interviewer to focus on the skill sets you can bring to the organization.

Accomplishments

Next, be prepared for the interviewer to continue the line of questioning. "That's interesting. Can you give me an example of one of your accomplishments?" Your examples need to be very specific and include not only what you did but also why you saw the need and how you went about accomplishing the task. The bottom line is critical: You need to show how you added value to the organization. You will be asked follow-up questions concerning the value added; so be prepared. YOU WILL BE EVALUATED ON THE QUALITY OF YOUR ACCOMPLISHMENTS, HOW YOU PRESENT THEM AND THE VALUE YOU ADDED.

Interview Tip! Value Added Accomplishments

You will be evaluated on the quality of your accomplishments, how they illustrate your ability to achieve the competency, and the bottom line contribution.

Be prepared to explain at least five specific accomplishments to illustrate each competency. Give appropriate details to demonstrate clearly, yet still present them succinctly. The best rule to follow in succinct presentation is the 60-second rule, which comes from sales research: You have 60 seconds to make your point to the interviewer or you will lose your listener. (We'll discuss this again later.)

The reason for having five accomplishments to illustrate each competency is that the interviewer may want to spend detailed time on one or two accomplishments, or hear a short analysis of all the accomplishments. The best interviewers will deal with your accomplishments and will bore down for details.

Following, you will find a series of examples of competencies and accomplishments for undergraduate or graduates with or without work experience.

Competencies and Accomplishments

Undergraduate or Graduate: No Work Experience

Competency:
> Broad, liberal background (Example-B.A.-Liberal Arts)

Accomplishments:
- Attended (college) and achieved a 3.6 grade point average.
- Nominated to Phi Beta Kappa honor society.
- Selected as one of 12 (from among 250 applicants) as a Presidential Host.
- Participated 4 years on Division 1 soccer team that won league and sectional honors.
- Volunteered as an environmental awareness instructor to 150 inner city students.

Competency:
> Demonstrated ability to solve complex problems

Accomplishments:
- Hosted 10 guests, from 3 different countries, when 2 other Presidential Hosts were unable to attend.
- Constructed environmental awareness curriculum guide and provided training to 6 volunteers.
- Created a data base, recording University's art collection.
- Created a business model and implemented a small business that self-funded 2 years of college.
- Conducted fund raising campaign that raised $20,000. for soccer team to go to Europe.

<u>Competency</u>:
　　Ability to participate on and/or lead a team
<u>Accomplishments:</u>
- Elected President of student government for a 500 student class in a close, competitive election.
- Studied in Florence for a semester and built a study group of 15 students from 8 U.S. and Italian schools.
- Selected as a team member in a Habitat for Humanity project with no prior experience.
- Won award for "Most Team Oriented" on the volleyball team.
- Led leadership-training program for a prestigious summer camp, voted one of the top 10 camps in the U.S.

Undergraduate or Graduate-Work Experience

<u>Competency:</u>
　　Strong marketing/sales background-B.A.-Business or MBA-Business
<u>Accomplishments:</u>
- Conducted direct mail sales campaign (1+mm pieces) to brokers promoting institutional products.
- Launched and strategically developed web site.
- Managed online "life event" consumer education program.
- Led and completed negotiations for a retail company with software and hardware vendors.

<u>Competency:</u>
　　Broad analytical background
<u>Accomplishments:</u>
- Worked on a $1+ billion sell-side transaction for an international oil company.
- Created an Offering Memorandum for a sell-side transaction.
- Protected New Zealand's hundreds of natural flora and fauna from invasive species.

Competency:
>   Ability to strategize with client, create vision and implement it

Accomplishments:
- Conducted business and technology due diligence on a potential partnership with a smart chip couponing vendor.
- Identified unique construct for keeping client interest high while introducing a new initiative.
- Developed division strategy focusing on sales to key accounts that doubled revenue in first year.

Competency:
>   Ability to partner with internal and external clients to achieve results

Accomplishments:
- Managed all communications with potential investors for mid-winter auction when the department faced a manpower crisis.
- Supervised the retrieval of a multi-million dollar piece of art in time for inclusion in an auction.
- Built community support and raised funds for a park dedicated to the 12 citizens killed on 9/11.

Now it's time for you to prepare your own competencies and accomplishments. You probably have many competencies, but the interviewer will only have time and interest for a few. Select the most appropriate competencies for the work you will target.

Your first competency will be the work you have targeted—if you have targeted a sales or marketing job, then be prepared to defend skills in that area. Your second through fourth competencies can be broader. Examples might be: strategic thinking, operations or execution, strong team player/leader, new product development, problem solver, outstanding communicator, etc.

As you construct your accomplishments be sure you include how it was good for the organization you represented.

Competencies and Accomplishments Worksheet

Competency 1:

_____

_____

Accomplishments:

1. _____

_____

2. _____

_____

3. _____

_____

4. _____

_____

5. _____

_____

Competency 2:

_____

_____

_____

Accomplishments:

1. _____

_____

2. _____

_____

3. _____

_____

4. _____

_____

5. _____

_____

Competency 3:

_____

_____

_____

Accomplishments:

1. _____

_____

2. _____

_____

3. _____

_____

4. _____

_____

5. _____

_____

What Makes You Unique

Once you have completed your competencies and accomplishments, spend some time on the question, "What makes you unique?" When you can answer this question well, you will be well ahead of the competition.

Suppose, for example, that you wanted to work for an international company and, in response to that question, you said, "I believe my international studies major, ability to speak three languages, and extensive international travel make me unique." Or, suppose you were interviewing for a job in the FBI or CIA where you knew they needed analytical skills, risk taking skills, and a perfectly clean record. Your answer might be, "I believe that my computer science major, my interest in sky diving, and the fact that I'm an Eagle Scout, make me unique."

Ideal Job

Once you have identified your key competencies, the next step is to define an ideal job. If you are single and just out of school, you may have few constraints and are able to live and work wherever you want. If you have a family, then circumstances may dictate that you live in a certain area of the country, or add other constraints to your job search.

Defining an ideal job creates a sounding board against which you will be able to compare real jobs as they surface. You may want to ask yourself the following questions about your life and career goals, which will serve as a statement of your ideal job.

Career Questions
- How important is it to you to work in one of the most prestigious companies in an industry?

  _____

- How important is it to you to work in an industry known for its fast pace and long hours (which could include weekend work?)

  _____

- How important is it to you to work for the department or area that drives the business?

  _____

- How important is it to you to make a lot of money? (even if it is not much fun?)

  _____

- How important is it to you to work with extremely smart people who will constantly challenge you?

  _____

- How important is it for you to be comfortable with the products and/or services of the company who hires you (would it bother you to work in cigarette or alcohol sales, private detective work to recoup overdue lease payments?)

  _____

- How important is it for you to work in an entry level position, with others at the same level, where you will be trained and grow at the standard rate as opposed to working for a smaller company with greater risk and greater, and faster, growth prospects?

  _____

- How important is it for you to make a contribution relatively quickly and receive recognition for it?

  _____

- How important is it for you to work for yourself? Can you afford trying a high-risk/high-reward opportunity at this phase of your life?

  _____

- How do you define the right life-work balance for you?

  _____

Life Questions
- How do you see the work life/balance in terms of time on each?

  _____

- Does your partner or significant other work?

  _____

- What are his/her career goals and timetable?

  _____

- Is moving to a new location a possibility? Is a move desirable? If yes, to what geographic area?

- Do you have children? If yes, what constraints do they add?

Career Stage

First Position

If you are entering the job market for the first time, you will be able to concentrate on your prior accomplishments and potential. You may not have experience, but you have a lot of abilities that organizations need to maintain a vitality. You are a recent graduate with new learning, energy, potential, and excitement, as well as inquisitiveness, creativity, and a new point of view. These are ingredients that are essential to any organization. Make sure you talk about these assets in an interview.

We have to make a point about the enthusiasm of youth. *Don't underestimate the power of this characteristic.* Sell the fact that you have always been a positive person with lots of energy and drive. Jonah, a personal friend, is president and CEO of his own business. He tells the story of hiring two young engineers for his environmental (air and water) company. Within a few weeks, the engineering department demonstrated an enthusiasm and sense of fun that Jonah hadn't seen in years. When Jonah told us the story, his eyes sparked, and it was obvious he was excited about what was happening.

Future Positions

Even with experience, there are virtually no positions where a candidate has a skill set, competencies, and accomplishments that are a perfect match for a position. Suppose you are interested in a position in the same industry and functional area as a previous job (perhaps for a company with a better reputation than your previous one.) You might, for example, have *experience* in 70 to 80 percent of what the job requires. Your focus for the 70 to 80 percent would be in convincing the interviewer that your prior experience and accomplishments would enable you to perform the job successfully.

Then, there is the matter of the 20 to 30 percent you don't have. You have to persuade the interviewer you have the potential to do that portion of the job. In all probability, you have accomplishments in prior jobs that are close enough to the specifications to convince the interviewer you can be successful. It is critical to know your accomplishments so well that you can provide the right illustration at the right time.

But suppose the interviewer isn't convinced. Then you have to change gears, from accomplishments to skills. This is typically one level deeper into your reservoir of success. Skills can be used effectively to illustrate your abilities at a broader level than a specific accomplishment. Consequently, "supervising" could be done in conjunction with a political campaign, a baseball league schedule, a conference or a project. "Negotiating" could focus on a dispute among college friends, a place to hold a wedding reception, labor relations, or purchasing a major casino/hotel. The more you can demonstrate how your skills can help you be successful in performing the 20 to 30 percent of the job you haven't done before, the more persuasive you are in the interview.

Interview Tip! The Extra 20-30 Percent
The more your can demonstrate how your skills can help you do the 20-30 percent of the job you haven't done before, the more persuasive you are in the interview.

Career Change

Even if you decide to undertake a major change, the process we described above will serve you well. Let's say, for example, you want to leave consulting and enter the not for profit field to have more quality time with your family. Let's say that not for profit would use 20 to 30 percent of your prior experience (convincing a client to buy) and 70 to 80 percent would be new.

First, you need to defend your ability to perform the 20 to 30 percent by citing pertinent accomplishments in that arena. The 70 to 80 percent of the new job responsibility represents an opportunity to sell the interviewer on your potential. You have to persuade the interviewer the skills you have attained throughout your business career and life can assist you in performing the job successfully. Changes like this usually occur when the interviewer with the hiring authority "falls in love" (in a business sense) with the applicant and feels the applicant could work effectively and successfully with him to accomplish the goals of the business.

The "falling in love" process occurs because the interviewer bonds with you and feels you can be successful.

Interview Tip! Business Accomplishments
Always have more academic and/or business success stories than you will need.

Summary

An important aspect of intellectual preparation is examining your competencies and accomplishments and deciding on a path to an ideal job. Specifically:

- Define your key competencies.
- List five accomplishments to defend each competency (including how each affected the bottom line.)
- Define what makes you unique.
- Decide upon a path and an ideal job (this may change numerous times during your career.)
- Analyze the underlying skills that have helped you to be successful.
- Think about how you will present your competencies, accomplishments, and potential when seeking a first job or a career change.

Step 4: The Resume

Building a résumé is about creating your primary marketing document. Throughout life, most of us have been taught "to be a good team player," or have heard "your accomplishments will speak for themselves." When approaching the job market, this logic no longer applies.

Winning the job you want places you in a highly competitive situation and you must present yourself in the best possible manner. Far too many people think of the résumé as a necessary evil, a requirement for human resources and the personnel file, and they think of it as something to be developed quickly and effortlessly. After all, they think, "The résumé doesn't get me the job."

The fallacy is thinking that the résumé and the job interview are mutually exclusive. This is absolutely incorrect. A well-constructed resume will help you get in the door; the focus of the interview will center on the accomplishments and experiences you've included in the résumé. The resume, then, becomes a critical means of preparing for a killer interview.

The thought process you use will help you force rank your accomplishments so you will only have room for your best. Furthermore, you will need to analyze each accomplishment in detail as you did in "Assess Your Competencies and Accomplishments." This detailed analysis enables you to lock each accomplishment into your memory system to be called on when you are being interviewed.

Elements of the Resume

Building a résumé is like doing a puzzle in that you are trying to get as much information on one page as possible (Note: executives prefer short, but informative résumés.) Type sizes of 12, 11 or 10 are ideal. Below 10 is too difficult to read. There is some flexibility in the font but it should be blocked and easily read. Times New Roman, for example, fits that description. You can make decisions regarding single or double spacing at certain points as you build the résumé.

The basic elements of the résumé include:
- A heading.
- Profile or summary (optional.)
- Education.

- Experience.
- Additional Experience (including Military Experience, if any.)
- Special or technical skills (optional.)
- Personal (mandatory.)

We will discuss each element of the résumé in greater detail and then provide sample résumés, which include recent undergraduate with no full time experience, undergraduate with full time experience, advanced degree graduate with full time experience between the undergraduate and advanced degree, and advanced degree graduate with full time experience after the advanced degree.

Heading
- Provides personal information and how you can be reached.
- Name, address, telephone number(s,) e-mail address.

Profile or Summary
- This is a future oriented statement that tells the reader your job function or intended job function and your key competencies. You are telling your potential employer the skill sets you will bring to their company.

Education
- Note: Education comes before Experience *only* when you are receiving an undergraduate degree and have no full time experience. Once you have full time employment then Education comes *after* Experience.
- Name of school, degree, major, years of attendance.
- Additional information—this could be grade point average, academic honors (honor society,) college honors (student government, art exhibit,) sports (soccer,) activities (glee club, orchestra, acting,) etc.
- Internships.
- Note: the ability to perform academically *and* in extracurricular activities demonstrates energy, drive, passion, ability to multi-task etc.

Experience
- Full time experience, summer internships, and interesting part time assignments.
- Company name (bold and capitalized,) job title (bold and underlined,) dates of employment at the company and at each job with the company.

- Job description is one or two lines and falls directly under the title.
- Accomplishments—bulleted accomplishments are indented and are written as follows: Action verbs in the past tense, the accomplishment, quantification of how it was good for the company.

Additional Experience (written in the same manner as the Experience section)
- Experience that may be different than your other experience, yet shows a set of skills (waiter or waitress.)
- Activities/Leadership Experience.
- Sports, research, music, interest groups.
- Military Experience.
- Note: if you have military experience, you should have this section. Many senior executives either have military experience or are highly patriotic.

Special or Technical skills
- Can be listed in paragraph form or bulleted.

Personal
- Great opportunity to tell the interviewer what you enjoy.
- Interests include triathlons, historical novels, chess, etc.
- Activities with others: Habitat for Humanity, Big Brother/Big Sister, etc.

Sample résumés are found after the descriptions. **Your objective: build your résumé.**

Heading

The heading provides your personal information and the best ways to reach you. It should include your name, address, telephone number(s,) and e-mail. It is important that this information does not change while you are involved in a job search. Since building the résumé is about efficiency of space, there are a number of possibilities for you to consider. The classic heading, if you have the room, is:

John H. Doe
32 Smith Street
Jonesville, CA 34567
(Cell) 304-567-8910
john.doe@aol.com

Other possibilities, to save space, include:

John H. Doe

32 Smith Street   (Cell) 304-567-8910
Jonesville, CA 34567   john.doe@aol.com

John H. Doe
32 Smith Street, Jonesville, CA 34567 (Cell) 304-567-8910
john.doe@aol.com

Write your Heading here:

_____

_____

_____

_____

_____

_____

Profile Or Summary

Note: It is rare to see a profile or summary on the résumé of a recent graduate because you don't have experience in a job function and there is often
an interest in keeping options open. The profile or summary informs the
reader of your competencies and can be helpful if you have an idea of the
industry or function that interests you. If you aren't sure or have no idea,
then it is better not to have one since you only want to have one résumé that
will function for all potential jobs.

If you do not have a profile, you will still be asked for your competencies
in an interview. Remember the question we posed earlier, "What are the
three strongest competencies you will bring to my organization?" or "What
are your strongest skill sets?" Examples follow.

Profile (Recent Graduate)
Recent graduate with strong English language and communication skills interested in secondary English teaching position. Selected (10 of 200 applicants)
for the Nebraska writing project and enrolled in Masters Degree in English.
Recognized for planning and organizational abilities, with a desire to assist
students to maximum achievement. Able to build relationships with all students and to create a nurturing, stimulating classroom climate.

Profile (Created during Senior Year)

2010 graduate with strong sales experience. Able to meet potential clients and build relationships quickly. Listen well, analyze data, and present multiple solutions to meet customer needs. Provide follow through and constant customer service. Relate to a broad range of constituents internally and externally.

Profile (Experience)

High caliber sales manager with five years in sales and sales management. Strong general management qualifications in strategic planning, business development, and growth improvement in sales operations. Excellent experience in personnel training, development, supervision, and leadership. Goal-oriented with strong organizational, interpersonal, and negotiating skills.

Profile (Experience)

Motivated marketing professional with 3 years experience. Capable of creating highly effective B2B and channel marketing strategies. Demonstrated expertise in advertising and promotions. Consistently exceed revenue generation goals. Outstanding rapport building, teambuilding, and communication skills.

Profile (Recent MBA Graduate)

Capable MBA with broad experience in strategy development, financial analysis, and start-up environments interested in the cleantech industry. Accomplished in market opportunity analysis to achieve faster growth, more efficient operations, and defensible competitive advantage. Able to build internal and external relationships facilitating communication and alignment, resulting in superior execution.

Write your Profile here:

_____

_____

_____

_____

_____

_____

Education

The only time your education appears at the top of the résumé (ahead of Experience) is when you are just graduating from college and have no full time experience. After you have experience, then the Education section will follow Experience.

Education is listed in a reverse chronological order so that your most recent education is first. The "must haves" are the name of the school, the degree, the major (and minor,) and the years of attendance. From that point, there is some flexibility regarding the information you give and it depends, once again, on importance and efficiency.

Sometimes, for example, the grade point average, academic honors, course-work (especially if it is targeted toward a particular function or industry,) and study abroad or in a specific program are included. In addition, the high school may be included, although this is usually not done after you have business experience (an exception might be a particularly prestigious, or unusual high school experience).

Usually, activities or leadership experience, even if it is part of your college experience, is included in the Activities or Leadership Experience section of your résumé. An exception is when your résumé is extremely tight and you include them in the Education section to save room. Some examples follow:

Education (Simplest Form)
Vanderbilt University, B.A.-Chemistry, minor-Biology   2006-2010

Education
University of Colorado, B.A.-Urban Studies,   2006-2010
minor-Business
Dean's List with Distinction-Fall 2004, Spring 2005. Dean's List
Fall 2005, Fall 2006. Colorado Governor's Scholarship Award.

Education
Massachusetts Institute of Technology,   2006-2010
B.S.-Math/Computer Sci.
Relevant Courses: Microeconomics, Macroeconomics, Options and
Futures, Differential Equations, Linear Algebra. GPA-3.8/4.0.

Madison High School (Madison, Wisconsin)   2002-2006
Graduated with Honors.
Awards-Academic All-American, No. 1 in class, Student of the Year.
All-County Soccer.

Education (Activities Added for Efficiency of Space)   2006-2010
University of Michigan, B.S.-Economics,
concentration-Finance
Cumulative GPA: 3.85/4.0. Dean's List-2005-2007.

Study Abroad: Johann Wolfgang Goethe Universitat-Germany
Extracurricular Activities-Research Assistant-Management Dept., and
Member-Michigan Women, Crew team.

Education
University of Iowa, B.A.-Journalism and Media Studies   2007-2011
Honors: Earned full scholarship to Summer Journalism Workshop at the
University of Missouri. Phi Sigma Pi Honor Fraternity. SAT Math: 680,
Verbal: 710.

Education (With Graduate Work)
University of Texas, M.A.-Social Work   2007-2011
Graduated with Honors, Hann Scholarship.

University of Tennessee, B.A.-Social Work   2003-2007
Cumulative GPA: 3.85/4.0, Dean's List every semester.

Education (With Skills for Efficiency of Space)
University of Oregon, B.S.-Economics and Finance   2007-2011
Skills-Proficient with MS word, Excel, Access. Familiar with Visual
Basic, MatLab and JMP-IN statistics software.

Write your Education here:

_____

_____

_____

_____

_____

_____

Experience

This section, which is one of the most important parts of your résumé, is easy to construct because of the work you did in defining your major accomplishments. In the résumé, place your accomplishments under a given job in a given time frame. Let's say, for example, you had a summer internship for the summer of 2009. The accomplishments you achieved during that summer would be placed under that job.

You will note an order to your résumé much like the college instructions you were given to follow in writing an English essay. The résumé is written in reverse chronological order with the most recent job first.

The company name is bold and all capitals, the dates of employment typically on the right margin, your title is bold and underlined, the job description, if there is one, comes directly after the title, and then the bullets which are your bottom line accomplishments. List your most recent jobs and the **most important** accomplishments associated with each job. Below are examples of internships and full time jobs:

Experience
SHARPE COMMUNICATIONS, INC.   Summer 2009
Public Relations Intern
- Performed a range of duties for Dallas based public relations firm.
- Organized guest lists, venue options, and catering (to 300) for client events.
- Wrote press releases (published in *New York Magazine* and *Time Out*.)
- Critiqued layout design for advertising campaigns (Exxon Mobile, U. of Texas.)

- Developed marketing strategies for diverse range of clients (restaurants, Internet start-ups, architectural firms.)

Experience
METROPOLITAN LIFE INSURANCE COMPANY   2007-2009
<u>**Marketing Manager**</u>

- Hired as Management Associate and promoted to Marketing Manager within one year.
- Launched and strategically developed MetLife's web site. Coordinated the initial design and organization of the online version of the consumer education program.
- Designed and implemented an employee awareness campaign and policy for persons with disabilities.
- Conducted direct mail sales campaign to brokers promoting 15 institutional financial products.

Experience
DESIGN DEPOT   2005-2008
<u>**Store Manager**</u>

- Managed 3 high profile store locations in Pennsylvania.
- Supervised 10 store employees at Malvern location, which had largest profit margin for two-year period.
- Trained and evaluated staff personnel, three of whom became store managers.
- Increased market share by 50% through effective direct retail sales and special programs.
- Hired as warehouse assistant during college, while working full time to self-finance education and was promoted to Store Manager in a record three years.

Experience
ALLEN & COMPANY   Summer 2010
<u>**Commercial Real Estate Intern**</u>

- Created and distributed monthly newsletters to 1000 readers about NY real estate issues to increase the company's marketability.
- Researched NYC commercial spaces and spoke with building owners to compile information for 6 clients.
- Created presentations and meeting agendas for senior associates.
- Updated and maintained the company's contact list (thousands) thereby increasing overall efficiency.

Experience

GLAXOSMITHKLINE   Summer 2009

<u>**Undergraduate Intern in the Computational Chemistry Department**</u>
- Researched literature and formulated experimental plan for a comparison of various 2D to 3D molecular conversion programs.
- Began experiment, data collection, and data analysis (will complete study and write a paper on the results in an Independent Study in Spring 2010).)

Experience

FEDERAL COMMUNICATIONS COMMISSION   Summer 2008

<u>**Research Assistant**</u>
- Investigated media cross-ownership rules and cable television market development and presented findings to senior management.
- Analyzed market forecasts to support estimates of the market for digital content.
- Increased visibility and accuracy of premier web resource.

This is an example of multiple positions at the same company:

Experience

SOTHEBY'S   2008-2009

<u>**Public Relations Coordinator (2009)**</u>
- Received the fastest promotion of any Intern.
- Promoted to manage all communications with potential investors for upcoming sales when the department faced a manpower crisis.
- Served as full team member at all planning and implementation meetings in preparation for the multi-million dollar auction.

<u>**Intern: Contemporary Art Department (2008-2009)**</u>
- Researched artwork for the purpose of making estimates.
- Managed the retrieval of an important piece of art just in time for inclusion in an auction.

Write your Experience here:

_____

_____

_____

_____

_____

Additional Experience

There are times you may want the reader to know about accomplishments in your background that don't fit neatly into the "Experience" section, but help to present a better picture of yourself. Some examples follow:

Additional Experience
UNITED STATES SENATOR'S OFFICE   Summer 2010
Research Assistant
- Analyzed research data on the numbers of people supporting the governor's proposed sale of the state highways.
- Prepared speeches for presentation to 2000+ people.
- Attended 30+ state functions to market the accomplishments of the senator.

Additional Experience
OBERLIN COLLEGE SEMESTER ABROAD   Spring 2009
Conservation Intern: Tararu Valley Sanctuary
- Protected New Zealand's hundreds of natural flora and fauna from invasive species.
- Created an ecologically friendly living environment in the Tararu Valley.
- Studied the agricultural industry through work on a 300+ acre farm.
- Volunteered at a backpackers' lodge, led horseback riding trips, and managed the organization of the lodge.

Additional Experience
- Cape Cod Sea Camps, Certified sailing instructor (60 hour course.)
- New Urban Arts, Photography instructor and Student Mentor in inner city Houston.
- MANNA (Metropolitan AIDS Neighborhood Nutrition), Delivered 1500 meals per day in Los Angeles.
- Research Assistant on major biological study.
- Public Relations Associate.

Note: This last presentation would be used if there were a number of isolated experiences.

Write your Additional Experience here:

_____

_____

_____

_____

_____

_____

Activities/Leadership

If you are going to graduate or are a recent graduate, you need this section to detail your participation in activities and leadership experiences. Employers are looking for young people with huge energy who can energize others with their passion and enthusiasm. One of the best ways to asses this energy is to evaluate your activities in addition to your academic program.

You will want to show physical activities (sports, intramurals, aerobics, etc.) in addition to more academic and extra-curricular activities (President of honor society, teaching assistant, head of fraternity/sorority, etc.). Bullet your accomplishments as you did under the Experience section.

(Note: If you have full-time work experience and need to conserve space, you can place sports and activities in the education section.)

Activities/Leadership
Outdoor Leadership Training Program
Leader and Leader Trainer
- Evaluated, interviewed, and recruited 7 prospective leaders from among 84 potential leaders.
- Trained prospective team leaders in leadership, teamwork, and communications.
- Led student group on backpacking trip in the White Mountains of New Hampshire.
- Ran training sessions to help students, faculty, and staff groups explore collaborative leadership through the use of a challenging course setting.

Activities/Leadership
University Student Assembly
<u>**College Representative**</u>

- Elected by peers to represent the 3000+ students in the College of Agriculture & Life Sciences on the 23-member undergraduate student assembly.
- Represented the community and students' best interests to form recommendations to the Administration.
- Served as Chair of the Women's Committee and Liaison to the Appropriations Committee.

Activities/Leadership

- Captain of Varsity Soccer Team; finished first in conference.
- Science and Engineering Business Club: Director of Finance Group, Career Fair Organizer.
- $50K Competition: Team member of Risk Management Start up.
- Community Service Teaching: Math to 8th graders, Finance to H.S. students.

Note: This last presentation would be used if there were a number of isolated experiences.

Write your Activities/Leadership here:

_____

_____

_____

_____

_____

_____

_____

_____

_____

_____

_____

Military Experience

If you have military experience, definitely highlight it. It will help you get interviews and it may help you win the job you want. Military experience carries with it the pre-qualification of patriotism, maturity, calm under fire and many more descriptors that are too long to print here.

In addition, there are a disproportionate number of senior executives who are highly patriotic and would like to hire a veteran.

Military experience should be written in the same form as in the "Experience" section but it should be under its own heading as follows:

Military Experience
UNITED STATES ARMY   2004-2006
<u>**Lieutenant**</u>
- Served with the 1st Cavalry Division out of Fort Hood, Texas.
- Promoted to Lieutenant after seeing concentrated action in Bagdad.
- Selected for specialized weapons training and became team leader.
- Completed 12-month voluntary Arabic language program with honors.

Military Experience
UNITED STATES ARMY SPECIAL OPERATIONS   2005-2007
COMMAND
<u>**Warrant Officer-5th Special Forces Group-Fort Campbell, KY.**</u>
- Mobilized Northern Alliance troops (2300) as a force multiplier in Afghanistan.
- Infiltrated terrorist villages and captured 2 demolitions experts.
- Received advanced training in communications.
- Applied unconventional warfare techniques to clear an area of Tigrit during Operation Iraqi Freedom.

Write your Military Experience here:

_____

_____

_____

_____

_____

_____

_____

_____

_____

_____

_____

Skills (Or) Technical Skills

Special or Technical Skills can be listed in its own section if you feel they are critical to your next job or you want to highlight them and you have the room. Otherwise, your skills can be included in your Education section or in the Personal section. An example follows.

Technical Skills
Computer Programming/Software Knowledge
- PERL.
- HTML.
- Scheme.
- Microsoft Word.

Technical Skills (Efficiency of Space)
Computer Programming/Software Knowledge-PERL, HTML, Scheme, Microsoft Word.

Write your Special/Technical Skills here:

_____

_____

_____

_____

_____

_____

Personal

Almost every senior manager we meet says, "I go to the personal section of the résumé first." Why? It gives him a place to start the interview, where he can focus on one or more of your interests and begin some rapport building.

The personal section is a great opportunity to complete a brief, well-rounded picture of yourself. Include interests you do for yourself and for others. You may also choose to add your language skills, language proficiency, travel, publications, and anything else you feel might be of interest to the interviewer. Examples follow:

Personal
Interests include aerobic exercise, tennis and skiing. Served three sessions on Habitat for Humanities projects. University of Colorado fundraiser.

Personal
Interests include competitive crew-race for the Club of the Charles. Language skills-Fluent English and German, Working Knowledge of Spanish, Beginner in Dutch.

Personal
Interests include horseback riding and long distance running. Volunteer in rehabilitating historic houses and enjoy residential real estate.

Write your Personal section here:

_____

_____

_____

_____

_____

_____

Sample Resumes

EXAMPLE: ABOUT TO COMPLETE B.A.

Name
Address, Telephone, E-mail

EDUCATION

Elmira College, B.S.-Business Management   **2003-2008**

EXPERIENCE

JONES ELECTRICAL CONTRACTING   **Summer-2005 & 2007**
Junior Project Manager & Junior Estimator

- Prepared "take offs" for the installation of video gaming machines and renovations to the clubhouse of raceway ($10mm).
- Researched project costs and presented findings to Head Estimator for apartment houses (50+ units), banks, and financial service firms.
- Evaluated 3-4 vendor proposals to determine the most cost effective offering.
- Assisted project managers with on-site visits to determine work progress, problems and solutions.
- Researched job site materials safety data sheets (MSDS's) and compiled them into multiple updated copies of material safety manuals required at all sites.
- Copied multiple sets of blueprint drawings for "take off" and job estimation process (30+ jobs).
- Performed clerical work including, organizing and filing job cost folders for project managers (5+ Project managers).

ACTIVIITES

EXTREME BOXING   **2002-Present**
Boxer

- Researched most effective boxing weight and determined it to be 147 or 154 pounds.
- Went on strategic diet to reach the prescribed weight (lost 40 pounds).
- Initiated a rigorous 1-hour training program of non-stop exercise including speed bag, heavy bag, double end bag, ring bag, upper-cut bag with intermittent squat thrusts.
- Learned to deal with and overcome pre-fight anxiety.
- Built a sparring training program, based on 3-minute rounds, that allowed me to learn the strategy of boxing and the conservation of energy.
- Prepared for necessary requirements of NYS license and amateur fights.

ELMIRA COLLEGE
Intramurals

- Won all-college intramural football two out of four years.
- Reached intramural softball championship (participated for four years).
- Participated in intramural basketball for three years.

PERSONAL

Interests include aerobics, boxing and sports. Enjoy history. Skills include Microsoft word, excel, power point. Volunteered at City of Elmira Animal Shelter (10+ hrs. per week).

EXAMPLE: B.A.-RECENT COLLEGE GRADUATE (NO EXPERIENCE)
Name
Address, Telephone, E-mail

EDUCATION
- **Hobart College**, BA-Economics; Minor-International Relations   May 2010.
- High School: The Millbrook School, Millbrook New York.

WORK EXPERIENCE
Hagen RESOURCES-Consulting Intern, Geneva Switzerland   Spring 2008
- Collected, analyzed, and prepared data for clients.
- Researched, analyzed, and prepared a report for the International Labor Organization.

CORNELL PRE-SEED WORKSHOP, Invited Guest   Dec. 2007
- Attended an economic workshop to help aspiring entrepreneurs establish their companies.

ROBIN HOOD CAMP, Director at Large, Brooksville, Maine   Sum. 2000-07
Directed 130 staffers my age and organized the daily operations.
- Coordinated the Trips Program.
- Organized and planned various trips involving 50-60 children daily.
- Worked as Photography and Crew Counselor, and Camp Photographer.
- Instructed children ages 8-15 on rowing mechanics.
- Instructed children how to take, develop, and print B&W photographs.
- Aided the development of children away from home for extended periods of time.

INTERNATIONAL EXPERIENCE
TARARU VALLEY SANCTUARY, Conservation Intern   Jan-Mar 2003
- Protected New Zealand's hundreds of natural flora and fauna from invasive species.
- Created an ecologically friendly living environment in the Tararu Valley.
- Studied the agricultural industry through work on a 300+acre farm.
- Volunteered at backpackers lodge, led horseback riding trips & managed the lodge.

SANTA REPARATA INTERN. SCHOOL OF ART, Student   Sept. 2002
- Studied art history, digital imaging, photography and an intro level Italian course in Florence, Italy.

ACTIVITIES
- Phi Sigma Kappa Fraternity- Founding Father, Treasurer, Organized Cancer fundraiser.
- Geneva Fire Department- Volunteer Firefighter & recruited 6 others to join.
- The Hobart &William Smith Newspaper- Journalist and photographer.
- Hobart Crew- Freshmen Eight & Junior Varsity Coxswain; Varsity Oarsman.
- Ranked 18th Nationally; 1st in Division III.
- Major Regattas: IRA, Head of the Charles, ECAC, NY States, Stonehurst, Liberty League.
- Hobart Fencing Team.

PERSONAL & SKILLS
Enjoy aerobic activities, and international travel. Languages-proficient French, knowledgeable Italian.
Computer-Microsoft office, adobe photoshop, SAS.

EXAMPLE: B.A. (WILL GRADUATE WITHIN YEAR)

Name

Address, Telephone, E-Mail

EDUCATION

University of Missouri, B.A.-English/Journalism   2006-2010
Named outstanding graduate by Society of Professional Journalists

Univerzita Karlova v Praze-Prague, Czech Republic   Summer 2008
Global Leadership Project, focus in Global Leadership and Civic Development

EXPERIENCE

UNIVERSITY OF MISSOURI BROADCASTING SERVICES   2006-2009
<u>**Station Manager, Market 70 Commercial Radio Station**</u>
- Managed $2.7mm operating and capital budget.
- Worked with FCC, business and corporate attorneys on a daily basis.
- Selected to supervise 10 departments consisting of more than 150 unpaid and 14 salaried employees.
- Implemented podcasts, a WBRU blog, weekly station-wide informational reports, website redesign, marketing intern program, sales intern program, intern retention plan, budget restructuring.
- Qualified in the use of Center for Sales Strategy Talent Focused program.
- Increased 2006 on-air revenue by 16% over previous year.
- Successfully implemented a $300,000 building and studio renovation.

UNIVERSITY OF MISSOURI BROADCASTING SERVICES   Summer 2007
<u>**On-Air Talent/Production**</u>
- Planned program content, talk live, and produced commercials for a listening audience of 120,000.

TIME INC. (TIME WARNER)   Summer 2006
<u>**Summer Intern:** *Money Magazine*</u>
- Accomplished research to verify accuracy of articles.
- Performed line edit function on lead articles.

ACTIVITIES

Missouri Men's Club Volleyball
<u>Coach/Player/Representative</u> to Big 8 Collegiate Volleyball League
- Created the Men's Club Volleyball program.
- Recruited 14 students to begin the program.
- Managed a $20,000 operating and capital budget.
- Taught over 100 students the game and built the program for years to come.

78 FM WIDR YOUTH MEDIA PROJECT
<u>Radio News Journalist</u>
- Selected as one of five youths in initial pilot program trained to write, produce, and edit five-minute news features about the community that aired after NPR's Morning Edition.

PERSONAL

Languages: Spanish (conversational), Mandarin (intermediate), exposure to French. Computer Applications: Microsoft Excel, Word, PowerPoint, westlaw.com.

EXAMPLE: B.S. RECENT COLLEGE GRADUATE (NO EXPERIENCE)
Name
Address, Telephone, E-Mail

Education
CALIFORNIA INSTITUTE OF TECHNOLOGY   **2006-2010**
- Bachelor of Science-Mathematics with Computer Science GPA: 4.2/5.0.
- Relevant Courses: Microeconomics, Macroeconomics, Finance Theory, Options and Futures, Structure and Interpretation of Computer Programs, Finance Theory, Linear Algebra, Computer Systems Engineering, Statistics for Applications, Accounting and Game Theory.

Skills
- Financial Tools: Bloomberg, Fist Call/ThomsonOne, TradeStation.
- Computer Programming/Software Knowledge: PERL, HTML, Scheme, Microsoft Word, Excel, PowerPoint.

Experience
MORGAN STANLEY   **Summer 2009**
Summer Analyst
- Priced gas and power indications for clients, wrote energy morning report.
- Designed model to test delta hedging strategies on historical data.
- Monitored trade blotter and volatility markets, manually delta hedged portfolio.

MERRILL LYNCH & CO.   **Summer 2008**
Summer Analyst
- Selected to work in Investment Banking-Technology group.
- Conducted comparable & precedent analysis, valuations for IPOs, and mergers.
- Built relationships with inter-dealer brokers, hedge fund administrators, and options market makers.

PFIZER INC.   **Summer 2007**
Summer Analyst
- Conducted online research on pharmaceutical industry to compare company's diabetes drugs to the competitors.
- Coordinated visits of 5 guest speakers to headquarters.
- Conducted interviews with senior executives and observed all aspects of firm operations.

Activities
- Captain of the Fencing Team, All-State honors in H.S.
- Science and Engineering Business Club.
- Student advisor to the Dean on curriculum selection.
- Team member of Risk Management Startup.
- Habitat for Humanity participant.

Personal
Interests include aerobic exercise, personal investing, and travel. Served as volunteer at food bank.

EXAMPLE: A.B. RECENT COLLEGE GRADUATE (NO EXPERIENCE)
Name
Address, Telephone, E-Mail

EDUCATION
University of Texas, A.B. Computational Chemistry   Projected: May 2009
GPA: 3.5/4.0, Study Abroad-Madrid, Spain

HONORS
- Dean's List with Distinction-2 semesters; Dean's List-3 semesters.
- Recognized by the Community Service Center as an Outstanding Student Volunteer.
- Texas Governor's Math and Science Award/Robert G. Jones Scholarship.

EXPERIENCE
ASTRA ZENECA   Summer 2008
Undergraduate Intern: Computational Chemistry Department
- Researched literature and formulated experimental plan for a comparison of various 2D to 3D molecular conversion programs.
- Began experiment, data collection, and data analysis.
- Projected to complete study and write paper on the results in an Independent Study class.

ORGANIC CHEMISTRY TUTOR   2007-2008
Private Peer Tutor
- Tutored four undergraduate students who saw their grades dramatically increase.
- Developed my own lesson plans and teaching methods.

TEXAS DEPARTMENT OF CHEMISTRY   2007-2008
Undergraduate Researcher (Work-Study)
- Worked with an undergraduate research group in theoretical laboratory.
- Incorporated relevant molecular modeling techniques in an independent study of the molecular conformations of ATPase.

KAISER PERMANENTE, DIVISION OF RESEARCH   Summer 2007
Undergraduate Research Intern
- Self-driven investigation of epidemiological trends in the dataset using SAS programming.
- Developed diagnostic criteria for calculating the prevalence of venous thromboembolism in a group of breast cancer survivors within the Health Care System.

ACTIVITIES
First-Year Advisory Counselor
- Aided 12 incoming freshman with the transition to college by preparing events during Orientation and serving as a resource for academic and social concerns.

Member-The Healthy Choice
- Worked with college sub-committee promoting healthy eating and positive body image.

PERSONAL & SKILLS
- Fluent in conversational Spanish. Enjoy running and weight lifting, Chopin piano works.
  JMP database software; C++ JAVA, MATLAB and SAS programming; UNIX and LINUX.

EXAMPLE: SOME COLLEGE AND WORK EXPERIENCE
Name
Address, Telephone, E-Mail

EXPERIENCE

COLTS NECK INN 2007-Present
Catering Supervisor/Senior Waiter
- Promoted within the front of the house staff due to willingness to "go above and beyond" in providing outstanding service.
- Selected as the sole manager, within 5 months, to plan, manage, and implement parties to 200.
- Managed 12+ staff members for larger parties.
- Managed parties for up to 50 people, without assistance, in an emergency.
- Built strong personal relationships with key clients.

WONDERBAR 2006-2007
Head Chef
- Implemented highly diversified menu out of a tiny kitchen feeding 200 patrons.
- Created indoor/outdoor dining service, hired and trained floor and kitchen staff (80 diners).
- Identified unique catering opportunities (Bruce Springstein's staff).

INDUSTRIAL INSTRUMENTATION SERVICES 2004-2006
Salesman/Field Technician
- Sold and serviced 6 major food companies (ConAgra, Universal, Orval Kent, Continental Airlines, International Flavors & Fragrances, Kedem.)
- Learned new business within 12 months.

HINCKS TURKEY FARM 1995-2004
Owner of Franchise & Catering Business (1998-2004)
- Created and built business, with no prior experience, and later sold business.
- Built the business from zero to $300,000.
- Conceived and implemented summer catering business, serving parties up to 500 people.
- Created first full-meal, eat-in and take-out business in Red Bank.
- Hand-delivered a turkey, after hours, to a key client whose kitchen caught fire on Thanksgiving.

Food Processing Supervisor (1996-1998)
- Selected to be a company representative to work with USDA inspectors.

Cook (1995-1996)

DELICIOUS ORCHARD 1991-1995
Cook
- Hired as counter salesman (1991-1992), promoted to Stock Purchase Supervisor/Inventory, Manager (1992-1993) and then to Cook: created prepared food business (1993-1995).

EDUCATION
- **Brookdale College**-Courses toward B.A. degree in Psychology & English.
- Additional Training: GMP OSHA training in product safety; Independent study in culinary services, food handling health and safety; Red Bank Boro-Food handling and safety course.

PERSONAL
Interests include hiking/camping, writing fiction and astronomy. Founding member of Interfaith neighbors-housing for homeless families. Eagle Scout.

EXAMPLE: RECENT MBA GRADUATE WITH EXPERIENCE
Name
Address, Telephone, E-mail

PROFILE

High-tech-focused strategy professional with an entrepreneurial spirit. Enjoy ambiguity and use storytelling to connect opportunities and needs with strategy and priorities. Care about good design, from business models and execution to user interfaces and technological implementation. Strive to delight customers, since this ultimately drives business value.

EXPERIENCE

IDEO (Helps companies innovate thru design)   2009
Business Factors Intern
Evaluated product strategy/concept viability as business-centered designer on multidisciplinary team.
* Developed a business case for making the supply chain more sustainable of a major manufacturing firm resulting in 50% lower shipping costs and for a new pricing strategy (double PV of profits.)
* Designed eight new product concepts that visualized solutions to capturing disruptive growth opportunities through user observation and competitive analysis (consumer goods comp.)

BAIN & COMPANY   2004-2006
Business Analyst
Worked as a member of client service teams to identify issues, design, and conduct analyses, synthesize conclusions, and communicate with senior management to maximize impact of recommendations.
* Analyzed and valued the target company's future growth potential in Europe and emerging markets as well as overall synergies with the purchaser, contributing to a corporate valuation reduction (paid -20%.)
* Created portfolio, R&D, and geographic strategic plan for $2B brands in a post-merger environment by working with depart. managers (raise margins by 5%, increase share 10%.)
* Generated pricing and brand portfolio strategy for a leading Canadian consumer goods company (40% higher gross margins per unit and a turnaround of market share erosion.)
* Built business case for a major consumer goods company to adopt a new distribution model that aligned sales incentives, reduced stock outs by 50%, improved price compliance (+5% margins.)
* Formulated I.T. strategy for a large employee benefits company and negotiated a $250mm outsourcing contract to reduce costs by 25% while improving service.

UNDERARMOUR (Manufacturer of high-quality, athletic apparel)   2002-2004
Marketing & Technology Manager
* Initiated a reformulation of brand position based on equity analysis to enhance awareness and adoption.
* Designed and managed 6 company websites (online sales growth of 93%.)

EDUCATION

STANFORD, MBA   2006-2008
* Net Impact Marketing Director, Private Equity club, Soccer Club captain.
* Led team that developed strategy for fuel efficiency startup (reduced time to market by 6 mos.)
PRINCETON UNIVERSITY, BS-Sci/Eng.-Computer Sci.   1998-2002

PERSONAL

Serve on the valuation committee of a VC fund. Avid outdoor adventurer: climbed Mt. Kilimanjaro, Mt. Blanc, Chimborazo, and a 30-day Alaska mountaineering expedition. Strong computer programming and database development skills.

Step 5: Research the Company

The best interviewers will probe for homework you have done regarding their industry and company. It is a sign of interest, and is also evidence of your preparation for the interview. You can be sure your competition will be doing research on the company.

Be aware that the company is doing research on you as well. Check your address on sites such as Facebook and Linked In and ask yourself, "Is everything on my profile something that I am proud of and makes me look as professional as possible?" If there is anything you or your friends think is the least bit questionable, take it off.

It is important to remember that human resource professionals are going to be extremely conservative in regard to your candidacy. If there is anything, even remotely in question, it is easier and safer to eliminate you from further consideration. There is no reason for them to take a chance on someone who is immature, questionable, or unprofessional.

Now let's explore the company. You may not be able to identify information about every question that is offered but do your best.

Specific Company Preparation

Sources
- Company Information-Annual Report, 10K.
- Internet chat rooms/message boards, Google.
- Networking with friends or colleagues who have knowledge of the company.
- Networking with college professors, mentors, etc.

Performance of the Industry
- Has the industry been growing over the last five years?
- Nationally and internationally?
- Is the outlook positive?
- What are the reasons for the trend?

Performance versus the Competition
- How would you rate the company's market share?
- Has the market share been growing?
- Who are the winners among the competition?

- Is the company considered one of the best?
- What positives and negatives can happen to change the future of the company?

Financial performance of the company
- How would you rate the most recent five years of sales?
- Is the trend positive?
- Operating profits?
- After-tax profits?
- Cash generation?

Management
- Is the senior management highly regarded?
- Is your potential boss considered a star?
- Are your potential colleagues "A" hires?
- Is the department one of the drivers of the company?

Social Responsibility
- Are the company's policies regarding the community sound and responsible?
- Environmental responsibilities?
- Health and safety practices?
- Are there regulatory threats facing the company?

Do you have any questions we didn't cover here that are important to you? Write them down here, so you'll have them for your research later:

_____

_____

_____

_____

_____

_____

PART III

The Power of Networking

There is a 75-90% probability your next job will come through networking.

- You build a network sales force of friends, colleagues and referrals.
- The RAPP networking system aids in preparation and presentation.
- Follow-up to your network interview is often where success is realized.
- Representing yourself well in a network interview leads to referrals.

Step 6: Where the Jobs Appear to Be

Suppose you were the head of a business unit and someone in your unit left the firm. What would you do? If you responded, "Who do I know that can successfully perform the job skills and who would I like to have on my team?" you'd be following the path executives take. You would mentally search your network for that person and call them in for an interview.

This networking is called the "hidden" job market because the position is not advertised or put with any type of recruiter. If you didn't know anyone, then you'd most likely ask your staff who they knew (tap into their networks.) That's why someone from your college, who graduated ahead of you, might recruit you or fellow classmates to come to their company.

The last thing you would do is to go to the human resources department to seek assistance in the "open" job market (advertisements, the Internet, company websites, professional associations, employment agencies, and direct mail.) One reason is that most people would be more comfortable hiring a friend or acquaintance whom they feel would be an excellent "fit" in their area. Another reason is that it is much more time consuming to wait for the process of advertising, screening résumés, and interviewing candidates. This illustration demonstrates why the probability is so high that you will land your next job through networking.

Networking, however, is only as valuable as the statistics that back up its importance. There is a 75%-90% probability your next job will come through networking. There is a 5%-15% chance you will land your job through advertisements (the Internet, corporate websites, professional associations, or direct mail,) and a 5%-10% chance you will land your job through recruiters. (Note: There are three kinds of recruiters: employment agencies, contingency recruiters, and retained recruiters. Generally, the employment agencies cover the lower or starting salaries, contingency recruiters cover middle level and middle management positions and retained recruiters cover the highest level jobs.)

Since networking is so important to your job campaign, we will concentrate on how to do it effectively. Networking contacts are people who will help you by allowing you to tap into their networks to meet people and gain information; they may actually direct you toward job openings.

From this point, we will call your network a **network sales force** since they will help you move your campaign forward. The goal is a constantly growing network of people who will be aware of your job goals, listen for opportunities, and pass leads to you. We will start with a brief example of networking and then discuss the process in detail.

Step 7: The Networking Process

It was Janna's first day in her new home in a Chicago suburb. Janna's husband Ron had just been transferred to the area by his company, and the whirlwind journey finally seemed to be slowing down. Ron was already on a business trip when Janna awoke and didn't feel well. She had a fever and needed a doctor, but she obviously didn't know any. When she concentrated, however, she thought of their realtor, Ron's boss, and the neighbor who had brought them some homemade brownies. Within an hour, Janna had an appointment with a highly regarded doctor in town.

The macro view of networking is that it is a **life-long method of building long-term connections that can become powerful relationships, built on mutual respect**. If done correctly, the partnership should be equally beneficial, and, when appropriate, lead to new knowledge or approaches. Where strong friendships develop, one partner may even anticipate needs of the other person, determine if observations are welcome, and, if so, engage in information exchange and problem solving. In this way, you build a set of powerful relationships and a personal executive committee that can be helpful in issues as diverse as career planning and problem solving.

Networking should be accomplished consciously and systematically, and should be underway long before there is an urgent problem at hand. It should be one of your personal standing agenda items, with stated goals that can be measured on a monthly, quarterly, and yearly basis. Some of the networking meetings will be planned well in advance, but there should also be an opportunistic element to your approach, based on awareness, that enables you to take advantage of unexpected situations.

The purpose of this chapter is to put a framework around the networking process to provide a strategy and system as it relates to networking for a new job. Any number of examples can be used to illustrate networking. When a young professional decides to live in a new city, he or she needs to build a network of professional and personal friends. A fundraiser for a not-for-profit organization needs to network constantly to be aware of new funding sources.

Networking for a New Position

The underlying premise of networking is similar to starting your own company. You become the CEO and the vice president of sales. You have a marketable product (your skills and abilities) because they have been successful in the past. You set the geographical constraints of where you want your next job to be located (East Coast, U.S., international, etc.).

What you don't have is a network sales force (people who will help you move your campaign forward) to help you to identify potential leads and opportunities; since outplacement industry statistics indicate there is an 80+ percent chance you will land your next job through networking, it's a very important component of your success. Consequently, you need to develop the largest sales force in the most efficient and timely manner. This sales force will generate the leads to connect you with potential bosses, job interviews, and ultimately your next job. Tangential benefits of networking will be a larger set of relationships and valuable industry knowledge.

There are several factors that differentiate your network sales force from that of a company's dedicated sales team. First, the good news; your network sales force only needs to recognize a potential lead and communicate the lead back to you for follow-up. That means each salesperson only needs to know what is on your résumé (education, work experience and personal interests) and not more personal information (e.g., you were the smartest person in your elementary school.)

Now, the bad news; the members of the network sales force have regular jobs. Each person, therefore, is helping you on a part-time basis. This means that any sales meeting or update on your campaign will have to be on a one-on-one basis, since it will not be possible to call everyone together. Furthermore, experience in networking indicates that you must be in contact with each person in your network sales force at least once per month or they will forget about you and your need for help.

Preparation

Networking is a critical component of any job campaign. Before beginning the networking process, you need to do some preparation. Initially, you need to be physically fit and at your highest energy level.

As we discussed, assessing your competencies and accomplishments is necessary content preparation to be effective in a networking interview. If this aspect of preparation is phrased as questions, they are, "What are the three or four strongest competencies that you will bring to my organization?" and, "Please explain five of your accomplishments to illustrate each competency, including how it mattered to the bottom line of your company."

If it is possible to quantify the results of your accomplishment in terms of dollars, percentage, or speed, it will be impressive to your network interviewer. It is very important to have a firm grasp of this information before attempting a networking interview.

With physical preparation and competencies/accomplishments behind you, it is time to identify systematically those people you know in various facets of your life who will form the foundation of your networking efforts (e.g., the foundation of your network sales force.) By leveraging meetings with the help of your friends initially, you will always be speaking with someone you know or someone who has been a referral from a friend or colleague. There are a number of categories of a potential network sales force, but those most valuable to business people are:
- Personal friends.
- Present or former classmates (high school, college, graduate school.)
- Colleagues from present and past companies (in every function, division and location.)
- Industry professionals (consultants, auditors, bankers, etc.)
- Friends from vocations or interests.

A key is to list them (you'd be amazed at how many important names you forget), and then categorize them by assessing how much help the person might be able to add. Define as highly helpful, somewhat helpful, and possibly helpful (a basic A, B, C or 1, 2, 3 system).

The system is imperfect in that some of the A's will be less helpful than some of your B's, although they are better connected. The written list, however, gives you an important starting point.

Start listing some names here:

Present Company or School
Includes:
- Present position.
- Past positions.
- Corporate personnel.
- Ex-company personnel.
- Customers.
- Suppliers.

_____

_____

_____

_____

_____

_____

Past Companies

Includes:

- Each position held.
- Corporate personnel.
- Ex-company personnel.

_____

_____

_____

_____

_____

_____

Industry

Includes:

- Professional associations.
- Consultants.
- Executive search-industry specialists.
- Investment bankers.
- Accountants.
- Lawyers.

_____

_____

_____

_____

_____

_____

Education
Includes:
- Undergraduate alumni.
- Graduate alumni.
- Honorary/award organizations.
- Extracurricular activities.

_____

_____

_____

_____

_____

_____

Personal
Includes:
- Family.
- Friends/neighbors.
- Social/civil contacts.
- Professionals: your doctor, lawyer, etc.
- Holiday card list.
- Fraternal/Sorority contacts.
- Religious contacts.

_____

_____

_____

_____

_____

_____

Note: After the lists are created, then you can code: A, B, C.

A= Most helpful B=Some help C= Least Helpful

After selecting friends and colleagues who will form the foundation for your network sales force, you need to identify a number of companies in the industry and the targeted geographical areas that could be of interest to you. It is not critical that you have the "best" companies initially, because your networking eventually will produce the appropriate list for you.

This data will give you credibility when you go to meet with a busy executive who asks, "Which companies have you identified as targets?" As a matter of fact, when busy executives are asked under what circumstances they will network with someone, they almost always answer, "When it is a referral from a friend, when the person is clearly focused on specific companies within my industry, or when I can learn some industry intelligence."

The focus for networking is not companies, per se, but the executives within those companies who potentially could become your next boss. Experience teaches that 25-30 executives in selected companies are about the most you can manage and that those companies can be, at a maximum, in two or three industries. Often, those two or three industries are closely aligned, such as a professional looking at a position involving creative and content in a company may also be looking at a creative position within an advertising agency, or a designer of apparel may also be looking at accessories or home furnishings.

It is imperative to note that when you go on a networking interview, focus *only* on the industry and function where the interviewer is an expert. Do not mention that you may be interested in other industries as well.

At this point you have identified a kick-off point (your friends and colleagues who form the foundation of your networking efforts) and an end point (the 25-30 potential bosses you need to meet.) The next steps are introductions from your network sales force to individuals who know the potential bosses or can connect you to them. Your behavior in the network interview drives the process forward.

Scheduling the Network Interview

The objective is to meet each person based on a referral and not a cold call. The referral not only feels more comfortable, it dramatically improves your success rate of achieving actual meetings. Assume that you are a recent graduate and looking for an entry level finance position in a company. Ted, one of your foundation network salesmen, has referred you to his good friend, Susannah. She is a graduate of your college and a consultant to a number of companies. Ted has told you he will call Susannah, and ask her to meet you.

When you call Susannah (a connection, even with a referral, often takes five to seven telephone calls) you will introduce yourself as a friend of Ted, who told you that she is an expert in the services industry, and then define the meeting. Upon reaching Susannah, you might say, "Susannah, my name is _____ and Ted suggested I give you a call because he feels you are an expert in the services industry. I'm a recent graduate and I'm looking for my first job. I'm interested in a finance position and Ted thought it would be great if we got to know one another."

Your objective is to schedule a meeting and get off the phone. Depending upon Ted's friendship with Susannah and his clarity in explaining the need for the meeting, you might quickly obtain a meeting or you may have to overcome a concern or two.

For example, Susannah might say, "Ted did call, but I'm extremely busy right now" to which you might reply, "I understand that and I'd be willing to meet before work, at lunch, after work or whenever is convenient for you." Under almost all circumstances, **you want a face-to-face meeting,** even if you have to wait a few weeks, rather than conduct the meeting on the telephone.

The exception for which a phone call is valid is where your referral is a good friend who lives too far away for a personal visit, but has a great network in your geographical area.

Agenda for Initial Telephone Contact
- Contact name: state the connector's name immediately (in this case Ted.)
- Expert: tell Susannah Ted said she was an expert.
- Define meeting: you are interested in an entry level finance position in a company in Dallas.
- Overcome objections: the intent is to get the meeting and get off the telephone as quickly as possible.

The RAPP Networking Interview
(Rapport building, Analysis, People, and Personal credibility)

Assume you have scheduled the meeting with Susannah; the framework for the RAPP networking meeting is based on four principles:

- Rapport building.
- Analysis.
- People.
- Personal credibility.

Rapport Building

We can't say it any more directly than this: if Susannah bonds with you, great things can happen. You have had years of experience in meeting new people and rapport building through interactive conversation about the weather, career interests, friends, interests, sports, or activities.

You have an opportunity to solve a business problem, but, more important, you have an opportunity to begin a new relationship. The importance of rapport building cannot be overemphasized. So, quiet those voices in your head that push for the business portion of the meeting to begin. Bonding takes place continuously, so the best communication style is an enjoyable, stimulating, interactive pattern throughout the meeting.

Analysis

When Susannah is ready to move on, she will say, "What did Ted want you to speak with me about?" or "How can I help you?" That clearly signals a move from rapport building to data gathering and analysis.

In the analysis portion, you'll give Susannah your résumé unless she asked you to e-mail it to her before the meeting. Susannah will want you to discuss your background with her. The purpose of this exercise is to place you in the business hierarchy; since you are entry level, this step is easy.

You don't have a lot of time to present your background, since research indicates that the average educated adult has an attention span of less than 60 seconds. **Your rule should be that no answer is longer than 60 seconds.** (We'll discuss the 60-second rule again and again throughout the book.) If the interviewer wants more information, she will ask for it. Some interviewers will want more background, some less, so you need to be ready to present your three or four major competencies and have accomplishments to prove your abilities.

Once Susannah understands your level, she might say, "You have a great background. How I can help you?" From this point forward, the transitions in your presentation become key. If you handle them well, your networking interview will proceed smoothly. If you do not, then you may have a struggle. Your transitions will move the conversation seamlessly from broad-based industry knowledge, to company, to people.

Suppose you said, "As I mentioned on the phone, I'm interested in an entry level finance position for a firm in the Dallas metropolitan area. I know you consult to some firms in Dallas and I'd love to get your perspective on some of the major challenges facing these firms in the finance area." That might lead Susannah to tell you about a few of her clients, the issues they are facing in finance or in general, and her overall view of the marketplace.

As you complete the conversation regarding the industry issues, you might make the transition to company by replying, "Your comments on the industry are insightful. Which companies do you feel are best positioned to meet these challenges?"

Susannah might begin to name some of the companies she knows or she may ask, "Which companies have you targeted?" Either approach is valid and you need to be ready. In the case where she asks you, you should have a list of those companies. In your case, you might have targeted large companies in a few industries. Susannah will appreciate this because it will immediately provide focus and she will be able to shape her answers.

What you want to know is whether Susannah thinks you have selected the correct target companies. Hopefully, she will add or delete from your list, and will give reasons for her suggestions. If she doesn't, you can inquire, "Does my list seem on track to you?"

People

Once the companies have been explored, you will make the transition to the third of the four principles: people. You might ask, "Susannah, do you know finance executives in any of those companies?" If not, perhaps Susannah knows someone else in the company who may be able to help you. **You always want to get a contact to the highest-level possible.** Susannah may not know a specific person in a company, but she may know someone at a competitor who knows the targeted executive well. It isn't always possible to reach your targeted contact directly, but one step removed isn't bad.

Quality contacts, then, are the critical component of the network interview. In your role as vice president of sales of your company, it is your responsibility to monitor the number of networking interviews you have and the quantity of names you generate. The specific goal of a single network meeting should be two or three quality names, in addition to Susannah. Perhaps the easiest way to remember and monitor your progress is a baseball system that examines the number of quality names generated in this manner:

- 0: Out (You networked to Susannah and if, at the end of the meeting she didn't like you, then you started with one name and ended with none.)
- 1: Single (You met Susannah and she liked you, but she professed to know no one else; then you started with one name and ended with one.)
- 2: Double (Susannah liked you and gave you one name.)
- 3: Triple (Susannah liked you and gave you two names.)
- 4: Home Run (Susannah liked you and gave you three or more names.)

Personal Credibility

The last of the four principles is personal credibility, which is a reminder that the most important contact is the one who is sitting in front of you at the moment, Susannah. The reason the network meeting must take place in person is because Susan must see you as a composite and not just an outstanding résumé. She needs to see how you present yourself and your energy, motivation, and drive. Susannah knows you want references from her, and that it is *her* credibility riding on her referral.

The voices in Susannah's head are saying, "_____ wants me to remember him and refer him to my friends. I will not do that unless I am convinced that _____ will make a good impression. I do not want to be embarrassed."

Follow-up Steps

Suppose you hit a triple and Susannah says she would be happy to refer you to two of her friends: Rafael and Elaine. The transition to the follow-up steps flows from the conversation. You might say, "Susannah, I really appreciate the referrals. May I have Rafael and Elaine's email addresses, phone numbers, companies, and titles?" After receiving that information, you might ask, "Would you mind making initial introductions with Rafael and Elaine so they know to expect me?"

Susannah will either respond "Yes" or "No." If she responds, "No," then it's probably because she is overloaded with a project or will be out of the office. You might say, in that case, "May I call Rafael and Elaine?" Undoubtedly, Susannah will not have a problem with that and you can call them immediately.

If, on the other hand, she responds, "Yes," then you have the answer you want, but you don't know the time frame. The vice president of sales inside of you will be pushing you to reach an agreement as to when you'll be able to call Rafael and Elaine (you don't want to call Susannah five to seven times again).) You might say, "Today is Tuesday; would it be reasonable for me to call each of them by next Tuesday?" If Susannah concurs, you have reached an agreement and you do not have to call her back in a week (win-win!)

Suppose, instead of volunteering Rafael and Elaine, Susannah doesn't say anything. Now the vice president of sales inside your head will be whispering, "Do something." You might say, "Now that we've had an opportunity to discuss these firms, is there anyone you can recommend I meet?" She may not be able to think of anyone at the moment. You have the option of accepting that, thinking you came in vain, and moving on.

Your alternative is to understand that Susannah likes you (you'll be able to feel that,) so you can consider her an additional network salesperson in your sales force, and you don't have to give up. You might say, "I don't want to put you on the spot. May I call you in a week to see if you've thought of anyone I should meet?" You'd be surprised at how often that is successful.

Assuming you impressed Susannah and she thinks she may have some future referrals for you, she may ask for copies of your résumé. Give her as many as she wants and ask her if she would let you know when she gives a résumé to someone so you can follow up with that person. Although you ask Susannah to contact you, it is highly unlikely she will, so **it will become your responsibility to check on any future contacts** during the four-week follow-up call.

As Susannah is concluding the meeting, you have a few final responsibilities. You might say, "I want to thank you for the time you spent with me today and for the referrals. Would you mind if I called you in about four weeks to let you know about my meetings with them?"

Then, as a final note, you could ask Susannah to refer you if she hears of a position that suits your background and competencies. You could say, "If you hear of someone who needs a finance person with excellent skills, who partners extremely well with colleagues, and who is a problem solver, I'd appreciate it if you would refer me. This has been a great meeting. Thanks again for your time." You underscore your three competencies at the end since Susannah will only be able to remember three or four things about you in short-term memory.

In summary, quality contacts that can connect you more closely or directly to potential bosses are the critical component of the network interview. It is imperative for the network meeting to be face-to-face, whenever possible, because Susannah needs to gain a total sense of you, and not just a snapshot of your education and experience as found on your résumé.

She will not join your network sales force and refer you to her friends and colleagues if there is any chance she will be embarrassed by you. She will be particularly impressed if you come to the meeting totally organized, with a written agenda, your targeted network companies listed, and at least 10 résumés. Finally, a network meeting is aimed at securing your next position. If, at any point, Susannah says, "I really like your background; could you be interested in working here?" the answer is, "Absolutely," and the network meeting is over, but the job interview begins.

Now here's a summary chart for you to refer to:

The RAPP Networking Interview

Rapport Building
- Personal bonding: if Susannah likes you, great things can happen.
- DO NOT CUT OFF RAPPORT BUILDING—Susannah will do that herself.
- Transition: Susannah will make it by saying something like, "What did Ted want you to speak with me about?" or "How can I help you?"

Analysis
- Career history: present résumé in 60 seconds or less.
- Competencies and accomplishments: be prepared to present if Susannah is interested.
- Transition: You might say, "As I mentioned on the phone, I'm interested in a position as an entry level finance professional for a company in Dallas. I know you consult to many firms, and I'd love to get your perspective on some of the major challenges facing these firms."

Industry
- Focus only on Susannah's industry and function.
- Industry intelligence: learn as much as you can and share what you have learned.
- Transition: You could ask, "What companies are best positioned to meet these challenges?"

Companies
- Target companies: be prepared to hand Susannah a list of companies and people you have targeted.
- Interviewer's input: encourage Susannah to add to or delete from the list.
- Transition: You might say, "Do you know a finance executive personally in any of the companies on my list?"

People
- Generating network contacts.
- Contacts: does Susannah know any finance executives in companies on the list?
- Goal: 2-3 quality names per meeting, including Susannah.
- Baseball evaluation system or create your own.
- Transition (to the Follow-up Steps): Susannah might say, "I have two people for you to meet, Rafael and Elaine."

Personal Credibility
- Impression.
- You want Susannah to join your sales force. She will not refer you to any of her friends unless she is convinced you have credibility and will make a good impression. She doesn't want to be embarrassed.

Follow-up Steps
- Referral.
- Information: get name, email address, telephone, company, title of referral.
- Contact: who is going to call them? When?
- Resumes: did you leave résumés for Susan?
- Call back: get permission to call Susannah in approximately four weeks.
- Competencies: as you leave, remind Susannah of your competencies. You might say, "This has been a great meeting. Thank you. If you hear of someone who needs an entry level finance

professional with excellent skills, who partners extremely well with colleagues, and who is an excellent problem solver, I'd appreciate it if you would refer me."

After the meeting, write a thank you note or e-mail to Susannah within five business days from the time of the interview to thank her. You should call Susannah within a month to let her know how your meetings went with her referrals and to remain on her radar screen. Subsequent calls should also be made to each person in your network sales force once a month.

The Thank You Letter

You have five business days to have a thank-you note on the interviewer's desk (or email inbox) before you lose the effect of the letter. The form of the note is a judgment call on your part. Is the most effective means of communicating with Susannah a handwritten letter, a word-processed letter, or an e-mail? It should be kept to one side of a page.

Since this is a combined thank you and marketing letter, there are three or four potential paragraphs. The first paragraph is a personal thank you for the meeting so it will pass through the gatekeeper (administrative assistant) and reach Susannah.

The second paragraph is a marketing opportunity. Re-state one or more concepts where you and Susannah agreed on an approach, product, or methodology. You never know when Susannah will need help and you want her to think of you.

The third paragraph is an opportunity to discuss any of your skill sets not mentioned in the meeting. The last paragraph is your closing which might conclude, "I'll call you in approximately four weeks to let you know about my meetings with Rafael and Elaine."

The four-week follow-up telephone call is your one-on-one sales meeting, keeping Susannah motivated to remain in your network sales force. Four weeks, as we discussed, is both respectful of her time and sufficient to have her keep you front of mind, and in your sales force. After the pleasantries, there are three main agenda items. They are:
- Inform Susannah how your meetings went with Rafael and Elaine (Note: if you have met with Rafael but not Elaine, so much the better—your meeting with Elaine can be the subject of next month's follow up call.)

- Ask whether Susannah has given your résumé to anyone else and determine whether it is appropriate to follow-up personally.
- Ask Susannah whether she has thought of anyone else you should meet.

Managing Your Networking Schedule

A reasonable way to manage your networking efforts, assuming you have full time to put into the effort, is to think of the day in two blocks, morning and afternoon, creating a 10-block week. Many effective executives have found that it is efficient to schedule planning time in two of the blocks. Planning is time spent on the phone setting up face-to-face networking meetings over the next two or three weeks. That leaves eight blocks per week to schedule network interviews (or job interviews.) In your role as vice president of sales, you can manage yourself against the following standard:

- Visionary goal: eight meetings per week.
- Primary goal: five meetings per week.
- Unacceptable goal: three or less meetings per week.

It is very difficult to maintain the visionary goal every week, but the primary goal is definitely attainable. If you do not have full time to dedicate to the process, then you will have to adjust your time accordingly. At five meetings per week, with an average yield of two or three quality names per meeting, you should be generating ten to fifteen quality names per week. As your network sales force grows, the management of your network will grow as well.

Here's an example chart of a possible schedule:

	Monday	Tuesday	Wednesday	Thursday	Friday
Week 1	Plan		Job Interview	Plan	
				Network Interview	
Week 2	Plan			Plan	
		Network Interview			

Summary

The case for networking is overwhelming. The network sales force needs to be constructed as soon as possible.

Building a network can be accomplished systematically.   By making methodical networking a high priority, you increase the depth and breadth of your network. The process should be implemented by establishing a predetermined plan with stated goals that can be measured on a weekly basis.

The framework called The **RAPP Networking Interview** provides a strategy for approaching the meeting. It is based on four principles:
- Rapport building.
- Analysis.
- People.
- Personal credibility.
- (Plus the follow-up steps.)

A clear, focused agenda for this type of interview, seamless transitions to maintain the flow of the meeting, and a well-developed close are critical. This RAPP method, together with a simple, functional evaluation system, will guarantee success.

PART IV

Presence

The self-confidence to build a partnership with the interviewer.

- Make eye contact; give a firm handshake and smile.
- Assist in creating a collegial, stimulating, and interactive conversation.
- Demonstrate a positive, outgoing, inquisitive mindset.
- Be humble, but not self-effacing.
- Speak (only) positively about others you've interacted with/worked with.
- Demonstrate the ability to relate to senior management and all levels of the organization.

STEP 8: The Interviewer's Content Agenda

Presence comes with a price: great preparation. It is easy to say it's important to build a partnership with the interviewer, but it is much more challenging to actually *do* it. The challenge comes in your ability to be so well prepared for the content of the interview and the type of questions you will be asked, that you can actually concentrate on building the relationship with the interviewer. Content preparation gives you the self-confidence to present well *and* build the partnership.

The interview, from the interviewer's perspective, consists of:
- Getting to know you (or rapport building.)
- Professional content (the skills and abilities to perform successfully.)
- Personal content (the personality and relationship skills to "fit" with the culture of our company.)
- Selling you on the company.
- Closing the interview.

The typical interview is conducted by the interviewer asking questions and interacting with you. This chapter deals with interview content from the interviewer's perspective and the next chapter from your perspective. After being sure you are prepared for content, we will discuss where content fits into the interview sequence, and discuss human interaction and communication.

In the same way that an excellent negotiator should be able to represent either side, an outstanding candidate should understand what the interviewer is trying to accomplish and why. Greater knowledge of each role prepares you for any eventuality and prevents surprises, the scourge of any candidate. In addition, **understanding the interviewer's agenda helps you with one of your most important tasks: helping the interviewer accomplish his/her agenda.**

The goals of the hiring process are to fill an open position with the best possible candidate and, in the long term, to raise the overall ability level of the staff. The interviewer uses behavior-based questions that ask you to describe situations similar to ones you might face, such as a time when you managed conflict or had to meet an almost impossible deadline. The interviewer works to uncover clues as to how you think and respond in those situations.

Behavior-based interview questions are intended to generate discussion about your past successes and accomplishments, which are the best predictors of future behavior.

The great companies have discovered the more interviews with different interviewers, within reason, the fairer and more professional the process. That is why, even at the entry level, you can expect multiple interviews.

Nick's profile summarizes some of the competencies that employers seek in young professionals; following the profile is a discussion of the interviewer's Interview Criteria.

Career Profile
Three Job Offers

Nick was ecstatic. He just received his third job offer, and it wasn't the three calls that shocked him, but the variety of the offers. The first was from a large, commercial bank in the management-training program. The second was from a prestigious consumer products company in their marketing department. The last was a sought after position in Africa as a volunteer in the Peace Corps. Nick went to his mentor, a favorite professor at Middlebury College, to tell him the good news.

Dr. Esposito could not have been happier for him. "You'll be a great asset to any of these organizations, Nick. Why do you think you stood out to all three of them?"

Nick laughed. "That's exactly what I came to ask you."

"Well, think about it for a minute. What comes to your mind regarding your marketability?"

Nick didn't hesitate. "Middlebury has given me great credentials on my résumé, and I'm sure my economics/international relations majors and grade point average have something to do with the offers as well."

The professor nodded, "Go on."

Nick gave the professor what he considered one of his greatest accomplishments, saying, "I always hoped that employers would recognize the value of my being the Number Two person in charge of all operations at the camp for 300 kids from 15 countries. Last year the camp owner, who was my boss, was away a lot of the time."

"It was tough, but exhilarating, to handle every aspect of running the camp, and meeting every objective and timeline. In addition, I had to schedule a trip almost every day for 30-70 campers with 15% of the trips being overnight trips. I also supervised the entire camp staff, including a number of people who were the age of my parents."

Dr. Esposito smiled and nodded, but said nothing.

Nick felt like he was bragging, but he could see that the professor wanted him to crystallize his thoughts. "Perhaps becoming the first Middlebury student to join the town's volunteer Fire Department and surviving the hazing when some of the old time fire fighters weren't sure that they even liked college students was important, too."

"You're right," agreed the professor, "but there's more."

Considering for a moment, Nick added, "I was able to recruit five students in the second and third years and helped the fire company fill its quota for the first time in a decade."

"You're on target, Nick; now, how about your international experience?"

Nick spoke about the summer he spent in Geneva working at a consulting firm, and the summer he spent in New Zealand working on a farm dedicated to environmental studies. In the first instance, he learned lessons in finance and economics, and in the latter, he worked as an apprentice sheepherder until the farmer took his family on vacation and left Nick in charge of the entire farm.

When Nick finished, he looked at his mentor and said, "I've been doing all the talking."

Dr. Esposito regarded Nick with pride. "You've done a great job of answering your own question. However, I'd like to add some perspective from 'my side of the desk.' You've demonstrated maturity and character since your first days at college. I remember you well from my freshman seminar where you took the lead in several group activities and were respectful of differing opinions, even when the give and take got pretty heated. Your ability to stay grounded and balanced showed maturity for an 18 year old. Since then, you've demonstrated teamwork and flexibility as you've willingly filled a number of needed positions on the crew team."

"Perhaps what has impressed me the most is the manner in which you won over the long-time fire fighters. When you attempted to become a volunteer fire fighter, I had no confidence you could win acceptance. Not only were you able to convince the fire fighters of your sincere interest in their work, you were also able to open the door for other students. That was amazing."

"You've developed skills that are and will be appropriate for the business world. Today's employers are looking for smart, proactive people who get things done. A well-earned degree from a respected college is important; at least as important, and maybe even more so are attributes such as excellent communication skills, clear thinking, flexibility, creativity, ingenuity, and drive. You've stretched yourself, Nick, by putting yourself in new situations in international settings. Your majors and your grade point average attest to your intellect; your leadership, individual accomplishments, and proven teamwork abilities provide proof of the other skills I mentioned."

"Industries can change quickly; you need to stay ahead of the curve if you're going to succeed. I can't think of anyone at the age of 22 who has any greater preparation for this type of world than you. It doesn't surprise me that you have received offers from three very different organizations with exciting challenges. Congratulations, Nick, I'm proud of you."

Nick was, indeed, an excellent candidate and the professor succinctly summarized what employers are looking for, and will continue to value in the future. Recruiters from the best companies, regardless of industry, know that recruiting and hiring top talent is the most important function they perform, and they have established systems and processes to accomplish that goal.

As mentioned earlier, senior recruiters are discovering that the more inter-viewers, within reason, the fairer and more professional the process. The screening interviewers, either on campus or at the company headquarters, test for threshold qualifications with specific emphasis on intelligence and the ability to perform successfully. Hiring interviewers then interview for character, "fit" within the organization, results orientation, and passion, in addition to the ability to perform in the specific role.

None of these areas are mutually exclusive, so both screening and hiring interviewers will overlap to some degree. Nick's profile is on the cutting edge of young professionals; however, the take away messenger isn't so much the breadth of his accomplishments, but rather, that they showed motivation, drive, organization, and commitment. That's what fast-paced companies and organizations of the future will look for in a multi-faceted employee.

Interview Criteria

Embedded within Nick's career profile above are the core competencies excellent companies seek in their new hires. They include:
- Threshold Competencies.
- The "Normalcy" Test.
- Character.
- Job Competence.
- Results Orientation & Execution.
- Fit.
- Passion.

Now let's look at each of these areas independently (although an inter-viewer might integrate them as she questions you.)

We'll discuss the core competencies the interviewer will evaluate, possible questions you might be asked, and then present a case study to provide you with some unique insight into the thought process and approach of excel-lent interviewers.

Threshold Competencies: outstanding core skills and abilities
- Academic training—college, major, grade point.
- Specialized training or skill development.
- Experience (if necessary.)

Threshold competencies define the minimum standard or floor of the acceptable candidate. Below this level, anyone will be eliminated from consideration based on résumé screening.

The interviewer will probe to determine your intellect, sound judgment, evidence of key skills required to be successful in the job, college major, and grade point average. Depending upon the company, however, there may be an effort to dig deeper into intellect with requests for SAT scores and graduate school admission test scores.

Technical skills are important for some positions, which are proven through your college major, defined coursework, and/or academic sequence. In some cases, either prior internship or work experience will also be important.

Possible Interview Questions
- Tell me which colleges you looked at, and why you made the selection you did.
- How and why did you select your major and minor or concentrations?
- What was your GPA inside and outside your major?
- What were your SAT scores?
- What were your major extra-curricular interests?
- What else should I know about your academic career?
- What did you like and dislike about summer jobs you have held?
- Choose an industry with which you are familiar and predict its future.
- Please describe an extra-curricular activity in college that best defines who you are. How did you become interested, what did you contribute, and what did you learn as a result of being involved in that activity?

(Note: In Appendix B. you will find more potential interview questions which will help you to prepare for the killer interview.)

Career Profile
The Circuitous Route to Threshold Competencies

Carlos agreed to give a courtesy interview to the niece of a friend; being gracious, he scheduled half an hour on his calendar to meet Ali, although her resume didn't include attending the highly rated colleges where his company normally recruited. He began the interview by making small talk for several minutes, but he could tell that Ali was extremely nervous. She didn't relax at all during the initial rapport building section of the interview.

Next, Carlos gently made a transition by asking about her background, so he could help her decide on a path that might be possible. "Based on your college major and experiences, what do you hope to do?"

"Work for your company," she blurted. Since those were almost the first words she uttered in the interview, Carlos was tremendously surprised. It amazed him even more when she added, "But that's never going to happen."

Stymied by Ali's statements, he simply said, "Help me understand."

Taking a deep breath, she began. "I have done networking research and Internet research about your company, and I realize that the colleges I went to are not at the caliber of your normal hires. I know that you're only meeting with me because you know my aunt, and I appreciate your time. However, I almost canceled this interview because I didn't want to embarrass my aunt or myself."

After pausing, Ali summoned her courage, and continued. "Would it be ok if I told you about myself?"

Curious, Carlos nodded affirmatively.

"I am the oldest of four children; when I was a junior in high school, my father had a fatal heart attack. In an instant, everything about my life changed. We all fell apart. Mom looked to me for emotional support, and had a very difficult time making any decisions. That meant I played a significant role in raising my younger brothers and sister. Before my dad's death, I had expected to go to a great college and live away from home. That didn't happen. I got a job after school and dropped out of all the extra-curricular activities I had loved. The only college I applied to was a nearby community college.

After high school graduation, I went to work full time, helped with the kids, and fit in school when I could."

Looking intently at Carlos, she said, "I love my family, and I don't blame them for the different direction my life took. I finished the two-year program in three years. I did well and was able to transfer to a state college for my final two years. By that time, my family situation was under control, and I was able to go full time. I was accepted into the honors biology program and received a 3.8 grade point average in my last two years. I am hopeful that you will consider me, based on my last two years of school."

Carlos and Ali continued to talk for almost an hour. As the interview drew to a close, Carlos was candid. "Ali, initially, I thought this was a courtesy interview that was going nowhere, but your story shows that you've gotten a top of the line life education. You've also graduated with an impressive GPA. I'd like to invite you back to meet some of my colleagues." Ali thanked him. Within six weeks, and following a series of interviews, Ali was offered a job in the company where she never expected to have a chance.

An astute interviewer, Carlos was patient as Ali spoke, and was open-minded about her threshold competencies; he could see the potential value she'd add to the company.

The "Normalcy" Test: expected behavior for a young professional

Being on an interview team is a double-edged sword. On one hand, interviewers want to give candidates an opportunity to sell themselves, while on the other, they need to fill the position with the best person they can identify within the time constraints. Hence, screening interviewers need to eliminate candidates and pare down the list, and hiring interviewers need to make the selection. To accomplish the task quickly and efficiently, balancing tests and scoring systems are devised.

Most hiring interviewers use their own personal "normalcy" test, which is to evaluate if your appearance and behavior are consistent with their concept of expected behavior for a young professional with your level of experience. We say the interviewer's own test because there is no one style or format. In most cases, it begins right at the start of the interview, is informal and conversational in tone, and is broad and general rather than specific. The "normalcy" test is part of, and impossible to distinguish from, the rapport building that two people do at the beginning of an interview.

In the nonverbal check, the interviewer seeks data concerning initial appearance, dress, fitness, and the way you carry yourself. Tim, a college graduate, would not be expected to have the same quality of dress as Mike, a proven senior executive. However, Tim would be expected to have on a conservative, dark suit and tie if that's the company culture.

The verbal portion of the "normalcy" test begins during the "get to know you" or rapport building mode. The purpose is the same as in the nonverbal check: Does the interviewer find differences between actual and expected behavior?

Rapport building is a critical time for both the interviewer and the candidate. The introductory period lasts as long as the interviewer feels it is productive or time constraints allow. Most theory indicates that an interviewer discovers a lot about a job seeker, including attitudes, values, and behavior, by helping the individual relax and become comfortable.

Consequently, most interviewers spend time focusing on the candidate's personal interests or mutual interests. This time normally gives the candidate a chance to relax and become comfortable in the new surroundings. Suppose, for example, an interviewer and Kristina were having a conversation about skiing:

Interviewer: Kristina, I see that you have an interest in skiing.

Kristina: It's my favorite sport.

Interviewer: Have you been interesting in skiing for long?

Kristina: All my life. My father was on the United States downhill ski team, and he started my brother and me on skis at the age of three.

Interviewer: Have you skied competitively?

Kristina: I've won numerous championships, but, unfortunately, there isn't enough money in the sport to make it a full-time occupation.

Interviewer: You seem a little sad about that.

Kristina: Well, I guess I am. It has been a big part of my life.

Interviewer: Are you able to keep up with your skiing now that

you've graduated and are looking for full-time work?
Kristina: Absolutely. I plan to go to Vermont every weekend from October to March.

Those are simple enough statements: "Unfortunately, there isn't enough money…to make it a full-time occupation" and, "I plan to go to Vermont every weekend from October to March." They seem to be speaking, however, about big time commitments. Kristina didn't say, "a few weekends" or "a number of weekends" or even "most weekends." She made it clear that it was "every weekend."

That presents an issue to be addressed on the interviewer's normalcy scale. Has the interest gone past "normal" or "reasonable" and into a red flag zone?

Kristina has every right to her personal life, interests, and passions. Passions can indicate energy, excitement, and zest for life. Indeed, many employers look for employees who have participated in competitive sports because they know about dedication, commitment, and how to win.

However, what about the company and its needs? If hired, will Kristina come to work on Mondays and Fridays with enthusiasm for her job? Or will those days be mental extensions of her weekend? What happens when there is an emergency project that requires evening or weekend work? How about the two corporate planning weekends each year between October and March?

How the interviewer weighs that short dialogue may be the critical determinant in whether Kristina's candidacy continues or ends. The normalcy test continues just as it did in our example throughout the interview, with the interviewer making value judgments that reject or propel a candidacy.

At the conclusion of the initial "get to know you" time, the interviewer normally indicates that it is time to move on. Whether there is a clear signal or not, the emphasis shifts to business oriented questions. **You must remember, however, that rapport building and the "normalcy" test continue throughout the interview.**

Character: maturity, integrity, and values that define who you are

Character is a combination of a sense of self-worth, an inner self-confidence, and moral authority. For us, this is synonymous with maturity. It is easier to see evidence of character after you have been working with someone for a year or two, but the interview team looks for signs of character traits during the interview process.

Information comes from The "Normalcy" Test, listening to how a candidate handled a conflict, or persuaded someone to change their point of view. It might come from having the candidate describe the single greatest leadership challenge they faced, how they managed it, and the outcomes.

Evidence comes in the form of sound bytes, those little side comments that add to or detract from your candidacy. Additional evidence might come from a self-assessment of one's strengths and weaknesses. There are many elements to character. A few are:
- Maturity: ability to deal with difficult issues compassionately.
- Ethics: the standards of right and wrong; moral authority.
- Integrity: keeping promises; trustworthiness.
- Self awareness and self-control.
- Values: know what one stands for; attitudes about the worth of people.
- Transparency: an authentic openness.
- Resilience: ability to function at maximum efficiency under adversity.

Possible Interview Questions
- What makes you unique?
- Please assess your strengths and weaknesses.
- Tell me about a conflict that you resolved, involving you and others.
- What are your professional objectives? How do you plan to achieve them?
- What do you hope to learn, both personally and professionally, in the next year?
- What is your greatest personal accomplishment?
- What has been the single greatest personal or professional obstacle or challenge that you have faced? How did you deal with it?
- Please describe a failure and how you dealt with it.

Career Profile: Character
Strong Character and Values

Ryan and Michelle were completing an hour-long interview, the twelfth that Michelle had at the technology firm. She was among the top students at one of the nation's best colleges, and was clearly in demand. In addition, she was personable and seemed to have great potential in the area of business development.

Michelle felt self-confident enough to ask Ryan this question: "Would you mind telling me why you spent so much time on the subject of how I would evaluate the success of my work?"

Ryan smiled and told Michelle there were two reasons. "First, when you begin to examine what motivates people and drives them, you can't help but gain insight into their character and values."

Michelle was intrigued by this and asked, "But isn't it difficult to understand someone's character and values in a 60 minute interview?"

"Of course," he responded. "I do my best to find out all I can. Interviewing isn't a perfect science, but you can find out a lot with a few probing questions, followed by the willingness to listen carefully to the candidate's answers, and then use your intuitive abilities to look for the many verbal and nonverbal signs that tell you what you need to know."

Michelle forgot about the interview and was intrigued by the question. "How do you get at that information?" she asked.

Ryan responded, "I tried to give you a few thought-provoking questions such as: 1. How would you handle a dispute in which a client directly challenged your billing invoice? 2. Under what circumstances would you turn down a piece of profitable business? 3. Can you give me an instance when your goals and your client's goals might differ and how you would go about attempting to resolve the situation?"

Michelle was totally into the conversation and she asked Ryan for the second reason.

He said, "Well, it gave me insight into your intellect and the motivations and drive you'll bring to my firm."

Michelle nodded.

Ryan said, "How people evaluate their success gives insight into their personal motivations. For example, one person may say she wants to be the highest gross revenue producer in the firm and make a lot of money; a second person may say he wants to service client's needs and help them achieve their objectives; and a third person may say he is an excellent account manager with the ability to cross-sell the firm's products."

Michelle asked Ryan what he had learned about her.

Ryan laughed and said, "You clearly have the character and values our firm was built upon. You are interested in building a reputation based on outstanding service to clients, and that is what we look for in entry-level associates. You are certainly the kind of associate we are looking for, and I think you could have a long and successful career with our organization." Ryan added, "You don't have any problem speaking what's on your mind. I also see real new business marketing potential in you."

Michelle was impressed. No one else spent that kind of time on the subject of character and values. That discussion was critical in helping each person decide they wanted to work together.

Job Competence: the intelligence and ability to perform successfully and think and act independently

Job competence (and character) is the main reason people are hired to fill a role. As we discussed in the Threshold Competencies section, there are a number of factors that are considered. For new graduates, they include intellect (SAT scores, for example), college selected, grade point average, technical and analytical skills, and internships. For candidates with work experience, it would be intellect and actual work experience.

The best interviewers go beyond these criteria to understand "how the candidate thinks." With the speed of change in this world, no one can be sure how long he or she will be performing a given job. Consequently, demonstrating the ability to think and to be flexible will be critical in convincing a company you are the best candidate.

The way the interviewer ascertains this is by rating the quality of your answers to questions, which is evidence of your preparation, and the quality of your presentation of the information.

In addition, the interviewer will try to gain a sense of your perspective. Perspective entails being able to see possibilities and creating a direction. Many young professionals are only able to see the box they will fit into and the job they are supposed to complete. Some are able to see intuitively, understand the bigger picture, and have a sense of how the pieces of the company puzzle fit together. This includes the mission and culture of the company, as well as how the company makes money or provides services. They sense quickly how they might fit in and could be helpful to others.

Potential Interview Questions:
- What is your most significant academic or business success in the last year or two?
- Tell me how you set goals for a project you headed and what the goals were.
- What is the toughest roadblock you have encountered and overcome on the way to achieving your goal?
- Give me an example of when you needed to demonstrate flexibility.
- What is the most creative thing you have ever done?
- Give me an example of when and where you showed intuition.
- When have you set a direction for yourself well before acting on it?
- If applicable, why did you accept and leave each of the jobs you've held?

Career Profile: Job Competence
Related Experience

Steve had recently completed college and was interviewing for a sales position in a consumer products company. He knew selling new business would be a critical issue in the interview since he was not in a position to bring business with him. He analyzed his skills and was prepared to talk about his ability to establish rapport, listen, communicate, consult, persuade, and present. He prepared his lifetime accomplishments the best he could.

Sure enough, when he got to the interview, Rhea spent some time building rapport and then turned the conversation to sales. She was kind and said, "I know you don't have experience, so we need to look at sales potential. Could you give me some examples where you believe you demonstrated sales skills?"

Steve was ready and said, "There are four examples I can give you. First, I was the leading Boy Scout three years in a row in a fund raising drive. I was successful because I was able to identify 10 key contacts or connectors who led me to many donors.

"Second, I won the Presidency of the student government in a close, competitive election that I was not supposed to win. I literally went to groups of students to educate them on the issues and persuade them to vote for me.

"Third, when I couldn't find a job one summer, I bought large old milk cans, painted them, and sold them both at a roadside stand and from house to house to make money for college. I developed my own marketing materials to leave at people's doors if no one was home.

"Finally, I was nominated and selected by the college as a senior representative to meet potential incoming students and 'sell' them on our college. At the conclusion of the presentation and tour, I gave each student my e-mail and told him or her to call me with any questions."

Rhea surprised Steve when she asked additional questions about the Boy Scouts.

"Tell me more about identifying the key contacts you mentioned," she said.

Steve responded, "I was able to go back in the troop records and identify past scout masters and committee chairmen who were able to put me in touch with people who supported scouting."

"Creative," Rhea responded.

They had an excellent conversation and she clearly became even more interested in Steve when she found out he was an Eagle Scout. She told him he had done an excellent job presenting how his skills and accomplishments gave evidence of his potential to sell. She also told him, when she offered him the job, that achieving the rank of Eagle scout was one of the major reasons she hired him.

Results Orientation: relentless drive to initiate, execute and accomplish goals

Results orientation is the ability to produce consistently positive results over time, no matter what the assignment or degree of difficulty. It is a mindset that is about setting objectives, figuring out how to accomplish them, setting an operational plan, attaining the necessary human capital and operational resources, and achieving the objectives within the established timeframes. Interviewers look for the candidate who thrives in a performance based culture, and who seeks responsibility and accountability.

Let's be clear: every time you present an accomplishment, make sure you give the bottom line. What did you accomplish and how was it good for your organization? Quantify the result. Show the interviewer your passion for crossing the finish line, for accomplishing the goal, and for WINNING. Employers look for people who want to win.

Potential Interview Questions:
- What is your most significant professional accomplishment and why do you view it as such?
- What do you look for from each of the people reporting to you when you are managing a time sensitive project?
- Tell me about a situation where you had to make a decision quickly and act upon it.
- When did you accomplish a task with the help of others that involved attaining resources, operations, and a tight time frame?
- Talk about a time where you managed the firm or organization's capital well.

Career Profile: Results Oriented
The New Nurse

Janet was interviewing for a highly competitive nursing position in the intensive care unit (ICU.) She graduated from a prestigious nursing school and landed a job in the ICU unit in a hospital in St. Louis. Now she needed to go home to Redmond, Oregon, for personal reasons associated with her aging parents.

Selene, the key interviewer said, "Your credentials are impeccable. We know you graduated at the top of your class from Muhlenberg Nursing School and we have received great references from St. Louis General. Everyone says you went in like a veteran from day one. Your nurse mentor even cut her time short by 50%."

Janet replied, "Thank you very much. I'm dedicated to my work."

"That's clear," Selene responded. "The ICU, as you know, demands a great deal. You have to be an independent thinker and decision maker on behalf of your patients. In this hospital, we're looking for staff members who can also see the big picture and think independently beyond what happens in your area. Could you give me an example of a time you did that?"

"I think I can," replied Janet. "Shortly after I arrived at the hospital, the Chief Operating Officer conducted a meeting of our full staff to update us on hospital finances. She gave us an excellent report on our hospital telling us we were in the black. However, our sister hospital was running a million dollars in the red. She asked that we remain keenly aware of the need for cost savings, without loss of service, wherever possible. She asked if anyone had suggestions.

"When no one else volunteered I raised my hand and told her I was aware we were spending over $15,000. per day on a patient in intensive care; when we were ready to discharge the patient, it often took one day for paperwork to clear. I calculated that, with minimal changes in improving the processing operation, we could save at least half a day per patient times the number of patients. I assessed that saving at approximately $800,000 per year.

"Within two days, I received a call from the President of the hospital asking me to be on a hospital wide cost cutting initiative council. We implemented my suggestion and actually saved $675,000 in the first year."

Shortly after completing another round of interviews, Janet was offered the job. Selene told Janet the example she gave on cost savings was the edge that pushed Janet's candidacy over the top because it showed Janet's ability to see a picture bigger than her area and to help her employer reach its goals.

Fit: ability to forge relationships and work as a member of a team

Fit refers to the ability to join a company seamlessly and become a member of the work team. Two people with many outstanding qualities can be entirely different in terms of their fit. There are a number of factors that can influence fit for a given job.

Professional preference can include autocratic or participative decision-making; a team oriented or individualistic work atmosphere; an intuitive or logical approach to problem solving; a strong concern for the logic of a decision or the impact of that decision on people.

Personal work style is another factor. Are you aggressive or laid back; outgoing or introverted; flexible or rigid; direct or circuitous; scheduled or spontaneous? It is both the interviewer's role and the candidate's role to determine if this situation is a good fit for you.

Potential Interview Questions:
- Give me an example of your role in a group project.
- Tell me about a time you became the leader of a project and describe your leadership style.
- Describe the best climate for you and tell me why.
- Give me an example of an organization or project where the fit was not right for you, and tell me what you did about it.
- Give me an example of when you were client centered.
- What project have you worked on that challenged your communications skills?

Career Profile: Fit
The Budding Politician

John, the wily veteran of his Washington, D.C.-based law firm, was the next interviewer to see Erica. John had heard great things about Erica from the dozen interviewers who had seen her previously. Erica had great credentials; she had graduated from UCLA and had a law degree from the University of Virginia. She was easy to talk to, made a great appearance, and dressed well. In addition, her personality was charismatic, and it was clear she was a "people person."

As was his style, John spent a great deal of time on the "What do you like to do outside of work?" question. Erica indicated a passionate interest in politics; she had worked on political campaigns since she was 16 years old in her native California and had loved being close to the political networks when she had held several summer government intern jobs in Washington. Erica also expressed interest in outdoor activities such as white water rafting with friends.

The interviewer focused first on the white water rafting, asking Erica to describe a typical trip. Once Erica told him the basics of the trip, John had a series of questions. His questions focused primarily on the relationships Erica developed on the trip. Questions included:

- "What were the dynamics of the group at the beginning and the end?"
- "Did you deepen any friendships?"
- "Did you lose any friends?"

John spent significant time following up each question with additional probing questions and listening carefully to Erica's responses.

When they had exhausted that topic, John moved on to Erica's political and government interests. He asked specific questions, like "Why did you first become interested in politics?" and then followed up with additional questions that sprang from the conversation. John was particularly interested in what drew Erica back to campaign after campaign. The move to Washington, D.C. seemed to make a lot of sense, given Erica's interest in politics. John learned that every summer since coming to Washington Erica had worked either on a campaign or for a government agency. This, as Erica and John agreed, was great preparation for a career in law.

Erica recalled being amazed at John's ability to listen for detail, recall those details later, and then bring them back into the conversation in the form of a question that was penetrating and made a lot of sense. John spent some more time on the motivators that drove and excited Erica, and then they concluded the interview.

The next day, a group of senior people in John's firm got together to discuss their reactions to the candidates they had seen. When it came to Erica, the reactions were positive around the room. John waited to speak, and listened carefully to the comments.

When he did speak he surprised his colleagues by saying, "I really liked Erica a lot. She has a great academic background and is a very personable young woman. It's my opinion that she doesn't really want to be a lawyer, although she'd be a great one. She wants to be a politician, and that is fine. When each of you discussed her strengths, you mentioned them in connection with her political or government activities, and you were right. She continually selected those activities out of the choices that were available to her, because that is where her interests lie.

"Did you notice how her eyes lit up when she discussed the intense atmosphere of a political campaign, the rush that it causes, and the second-by-second decisions that have to be made? Do you think Erica is going to be happy working on analysis gathering for a corporate litigation case? How long do you think she'll remain with us if we hire her? I think the answer is, until the next political campaign calls her. I'd love to have Erica as a young associate in the firm, but I don't think hiring her is a wise investment of time or financial resources when we know it takes five to seven years to produce an outstanding attorney."

There was silence in the room until one of John's senior colleagues reflected, "You know, John, that is what makes you outstanding. You really mine down into a candidate's motivations as a way to get to know him or her. Your predictions about a candidates potential for success in the firm are almost always 100% correct."

"The reason we make mistakes is that we don't listen to what the candidates have to say about what drives and motivates them. I was sold on Erica because she has a great personality, but when you ask me what excites her, you're right, it is politics."

Erica went on to have a great career at a public relations and marketing firm that represented politicians during elections.

Passion: deep, heartfelt, authentic excitement about work and life that includes the ability to energize others

Passion is the fire and relentless drive to initiate, execute, and achieve results beyond what is expected. Passion clearly differentiates candidates and separates winners from losers in the interview process. It also differentiates on-the-job performance. Those who are filled with energy and can energize others move forward in their organization.

Potential Interview Questions:
- Tell me about something you are passionate about.
- Give me an instance where you had to expend huge energy on a project.
- Tell me about a time when you had to use your gut to make a decision.

- When did you have to overcome resistance from co-workers or friends?

Career Profile: Results Oriented
Real Hero

Imagine the shock of the interviewer who interviewed Jeff Blatnick for an entry-level position in his manufacturing company and asked Jeff to tell him something he was passionate about. Jeff's answer was, "I hoped to be a Greco-Roman wrestler for the United States Olympic team. Two years before the Olympics, I was weight lifting when I discovered several lumps in my neck. I went to my family physician in Schenectady, New York, who gave me the diagnosis of Hodgkin's disease. Within a month, doctors had removed my spleen and started me on radiation therapy. I was told I would not compete again. I went through all the emotional reactions you can imagine, but I did not agree with the doctor's assessment. I made the decision that I was going to beat this new opponent and wrestle again. I began to work out again and I endured the rigors of Olympic training while fighting to overcome cancer."

By this time the interviewer had completely forgotten the interview. "What happened next?" he asked.

"Perseverance paid off," Jeff said. "I made the Olympic team and won the starting position in the super heavyweight division. My biggest wins were when I upset a Yugoslav and defeated a Greek who bit me in the hand during the match. I won the Gold Medal with a victory over a Swede."

There was a long silence and then the interviewer asked Jeff to wait a moment. When the interviewer came back, he had three executives with him. He apologized to Jeff for asking him to retell the story but in much greater detail. When Jeff was finished, the Division President looked at Jeff and said, "Jeff, what I'm going to do now has never been done in the history of this company. I'm offering you a job on the spot. That story you just told us is beyond amazing. It gives evidence of so many of the characteristics we look for in a candidate, including having passion for life and work. I know I'm going to be proud to be associated with you."

Summary

The interviewer has the need to evaluate you in a number of areas. They include:
- Threshold Competencies.
- The "Normalcy" Test.
- Character.
- Job Competence.
- Results Orientation & Execution.
- Fit.
- Passion.

The quality of your answers demonstrates to the interviewers the degree of your preparation. Content preparation gives you the self-confidence to know that you will answer the questions well so you can focus on building the relationship with the interviewer. This is evidence of your PRESENCE.

Step 9: Your Content Agenda

We are often asked, "What's the big deal about preparation?" The answer is simple. "Does the interviewer have something you want (a job)?" Since the answer is an obvious "Yes," then we need to stick to the same content agenda we discussed in the last chapter. And, **since there is no perfect candidate, you will want to think about real or perceived issues the interviewer might have with your candidacy, and be prepared to address them.**

In this chapter, we will discuss some questions the interviewer will ask himself in order to evaluate you, and then we'll give you a Career Profile that will illustrate how a well-prepared candidate analyzed what the interviewer might ask and how she handled the question.

Interview Criteria

Don't forget; the major areas of concern for the interviewer are:
- Threshold Competencies.
- The "Normalcy" Test.
- Character.
- Job Competence.
- Results Orientation & Execution.
- Fit.
- Passion.

Threshold Competencies: outstanding core skills and abilities

Possible Interview Question: Tell me which colleges you evaluated, why you made the selection you did, what your thinking was about selecting your major and minor or concentrations, and what your GPA was.

Threshold competencies define the minimum standard of the acceptable candidate. The objective is to determine your level of business acumen and ability to think. The interviewer will evaluate you on the following:
- High School grades and SAT scores.
- College attended. Why?
- College major/minor or concentration and GPA.
- Knowledge, skills, and abilities.
- Internships or job experience.
- Business acumen and clear thinking.
- Alternatives to the normally accepted path to threshold competencies.

As you analyze your academic career, you want to evaluate the strongest and weakest aspects and anticipate what a savvy interviewer might ask. In the last chapter, we saw how Ali overcame the apparent lack of depth of her academic program. In this career profile, we see how Kumi overcame a slightly lower grade point average than the company expected. What are your academic strengths and perceived weaknesses and how will you respond to weaker areas?

Career Profile: Threshold Competencies
Two Majors

Kumi was concerned about his upcoming interview. He knew from his networking efforts that one of the first questions he would be asked would be, "What was your grade point average?" His grade point average was 3.0 and he knew that would be an issue. After careful consideration and some excellent advice, Kumi devised his plan of attack.

His interview was scheduled and he arrived in plenty of time. Once the interviewer, Mr. Trawin, met Kumi, they spent 10-15 minutes building rapport. Kumi was comfortable, feeling that they went past rapport building into some bonding. At the conclusion of the rapport building, Mr. Trawin told Kumi that he would like to transition to a business discussion. One of the first questions he asked Kumi was why he selected Michigan State University. Kumi told him he was a recruited basketball player and the team was a top NCAA program. They spent some time talking about the basketball program, and Kumi's role as a team member and as a leader.

Mr. Trawin then asked Kumi about his grade point average. Kumi told him it was a 3.0. Mr. Trawin said, "Michigan State has been one of our targeted schools. We have recruited MSU graduates and they have done well in our company. However, your grade point is lower than we would like. What can you tell me about your grades?"

Kumi was ready. "When I went to Michigan State, I knew I would be signing on for two majors, business and basketball. I worked hard in my studies and I worked hard in basketball. The basketball team traveled a great deal, and there were some professors who were more understanding of that than others.

"When it came time for the NCAA tournament, it was difficult for us to make our classes. We reached the final 8 one year and the final 4 another. I always had my books with me and studied every chance I got. There were a few classes where I was right on the border of a 2.5 and a 3.0 and I received the lower grade. But I never stopped working hard, and I turned every assignment in on time. I am proud of what I've achieved in both basketball and my business courses. Truthfully, I believe that what I learned from my basketball experience will benefit me greatly in the business world."

Mr. Trawin responded sincerely. "You've told a compelling story about your career at Michigan State. I understand your point of view." Ultimately, after a series of interviews, Kumi was hired.

The "Normalcy" Test: expected behavior for young professionals

Possible interview question: What is your greatest passion outside of work?

Interviewers conduct their own personal "normalcy" test, which is designed to pick up deviations from their concept of ideal behavior for someone at your level. It is part of, and impossible to distinguish from, the rapport-building phase of the interview.

The interviewer will evaluate you on the following:
- Does the candidate make a good appearance?
- Is her dress appropriate?
- Does he appear confident and friendly?
- Does she smile?
- Does he have a firm handshake?
- Does she have excellent eye contact?
- How does he carry himself?
- Does she have any unusual mannerisms?
- Are there differences between his actual and expected behavior?
- Was there anything on his Facebook or Linked In accounts that raised red flags?
- Are there any red flags about anything in her background that need to be investigated?

In the last chapter, we weren't sure if Kristina shot herself in the foot with her remarks about skiing. In this career profile, Sandra goes right at Kim regarding her concert career to determine if she really wants to be a teacher. What question(s) might an interviewer ask about your background?

Career Profile: The "Normalcy" Test
The Concert Violinist

Kim had reached a personal pinnacle when she performed with the New York Philharmonic at Carnegie Hall. The 16 years of violin lessons, practice, and concerts would always be a part of her life. She was also realistic enough to know that being a backup violinist was the highest level she would attain. Right or wrong, there were some musicians who had achieved greater success. Kim had come to peace with the situation and decided to pursue her second love, teaching others. She discovered that she had the personality, resilience, and patience to work with high school students.

She knew she would be challenged on whether she really wanted to be a music teacher as opposed to finding an orchestra where she could be first chair. When she went to the interview, she was prepared. Kim was fit, professional and well dressed.

Kim met Anita, the principal of the private high school, with a smile, confident eye contact, and a firm handshake. Anita welcomed Kim into her office and started the conversation by referring to Kim's achievements in the music field. Anita then asked Kim why she decided to seek a teaching career.

Kim responded, "I love to play the violin, and I have been fortunate to be recognized for my abilities. I also realize there comes a time when someone has to take a longer view of their career and I've decided teaching is the best way for me to remain involved in music, provide a service to young people, and provide a livelihood for the long term."

Anita asked, "Are you sure you'll have the patience to teach high school students?"

"I think so," responded Kim. "I've worked with students in a summer camp and have given private music lessons, and I enjoyed working with every camper and student."

"What about your concert career?" asked Anita.

Kim responded, "I'm prepared to give that up. I'm thinking about auditioning for the New Jersey Symphony Orchestra, but that wouldn't conflict with my teaching duties."

Anita prodded a little further, "I'm sorry to ask again, but have you been thinking about this for any period of time?"

"Yes," Kim responded, "For about a year I have been thinking about this, and I am very comfortable with my decision. Why do you ask?"

Anita responded, "I just wanted to be sure that your decision wasn't impulsive, but was well thought out."

That exchange was the critical part of Kim's interview. Anita had an opportunity to hire a great musician for her highly dynamic, and demanding, private high school, but she needed to be sure that Kim wanted, and was ready for, a teaching career. Neither she, nor Kim, would totally be sure whether teaching was for Kim until she was on the job. But Kim had convinced Anita that she was ready for the change and Anita hired her.

Character: maturity, integrity and values that define who you are

Possible Interview Question: Tell me about a time when you have been able to help other people.

Character is a combination of a sense of self-worth, an inner self-confidence, and moral authority. Character is difficult to assess in a job interview, but an observant interviewer can pick up many more signals than you might think. It is usually in sound bytes when you are explaining how you resolved a conflict, or when you convinced someone to consider a different point of view.

The largest opportunity for a mistake comes when you are not prepared. When you haven't thought through your outstanding accomplishments in your personal (as well as business) life, there is a much greater likelihood you will stumble through your answers and volunteer negatives about yourself.

The interviewer will evaluate you on the following:
- Does she demonstrate maturity?
- Is he comfortable in his own skin?
- Can she deal with tough issues compassionately (with tact, diplomacy and empathy?)
- Does he have an abundance mentality (there is an ever enlarging opportunity for everyone?)
- Does she demonstrate resilience or the ability to function at maximum efficiency under adversity?
- Does he demonstrate integrity to keep promises made to self and others?
- Does she know what she stands for no matter the cost?
- Does he reach out to others in order to give something back?

In the last chapter we saw how Michelle and Ryan engaged in a great conversation about character; in this career profile, we'll see how Sandra's outside interest is helpful. How will you respond to a question about helping or valuing the contributions of others?

Career Profile: Character
Special Olympics

Sandra and her boyfriend had both grown up in the same small city and desperately wanted to move back to Minnesota so they could be close to their elderly parents. Sandra applied to a large company 2 hours from her parents' home for an entry-level finance position. She was genuinely excited when she received a call for an interview. She felt prepared personally, learned as much about the company as she could, and had her interview clothes and extra copies of her résumé.

It was a long drive, so she went the night before and stayed in a hotel close to the corporate offices. The next morning, she was scheduled to meet with a human resources executive and at least one finance executive. She had been told the company had a strong public service culture and she might be asked what she did to help others.

The meeting with the human resource executive went well. Sandra learned her résumé had been selected out of a screening of over 200 résumés. The interviewer told her that her finance degree from the University of Minnesota was impressive and that the company had good experience with graduates of the school. That comment helped Sandra relax and look forward to the next interview.

Sandra was then walked to Vivek's office. He would be Sandra's boss if she received an offer. He was young, perhaps only a few years older than Sandra, and seemed somewhat uncomfortable. Vivek was formal and quite stiff initially, and moved to the business portion of the meeting immediately. He had Sandra's résumé in front of him, but had obviously not read it beforehand. He began the interview by having her give a personal and career history. Sandra was not feeling confident about what had happened to this point. After she finished, he went back to her résumé and eventually came to the "Personal" section at the bottom.

There he discovered Sandra was a volunteer for the Special Olympics. As he asked Sandra how she got involved, Sandra noticed a distinct change in Vivek's behavior for the better. He was much more friendly and relaxed, and wanted to know the details. It was clear that he was interested. A quick thought flashed through Sandra's mind about her initial reluctance to put a personal section on her résumé, and how much her mentor had encouraged her to do it. Now, she was glad she did; the rest of the interview went much better.

As Vivek was walking Sandra out, they had a chance meeting with Andrew, the Chief Financial Officer of the company, who was just coming in from a breakfast meeting. Vivek introduced Sandra to Andrew, and they stood and spoke for a few minutes. Near the end of the conversation, Vivek mentioned that Sandra was a volunteer for the Special Olympics program.

Andrew looked at his watch and said, "I have a few minutes before my next appointment. Sandra, would you like to visit with me?"

Sandra didn't know how unusual it was to have a meeting with the CFO.

As they sat down, Andrew asked, "How did you get involved with the Special Olympics?"

Sandra said, "My boyfriend and I wanted to volunteer to try and make a difference in children's lives and this seemed like a worthy cause."

Andrew responded, "It is. Do you have any special needs children in your family?"

Sandra told him that neither she nor her boyfriend did, but they loved the interaction with special needs children.

Andrew told Sandra about his ten-year-old son who had Down syndrome and how much the Special Olympics had brought a level of joy and self-confidence to his life that Andrew had never seen before. They had a great 15-minute conversation, which ended with Andrew walking Sandra to the door. Later, when Andrew and Vivek discussed the candidates who had been interviewed, it was Sandra who was at the top of the list. Sandra received a call shortly thereafter with a job offer which she was happy to accept.

Job Competence: the intelligence and ability to perform successfully, and to think and act independently

Possible Interview Question: What was your greatest internship or work related accomplishment in the past 2 years?

The interviewer is looking for evidence that, not only do you have intelligence and the ability to think, but also that you will be able to apply that intelligence in a business setting. No executive can completely predict where a new hire will be in a year or two within the company's divisions, so the ability to see the big picture and flexibility are key skill sets.

The interviewer will look for a set of skills that include:
- Relationship skills & teamwork.
- Communication skills.
- Problem solving abilities.
- Drive to succeed.
- Client-centeredness.
- Analytical & computer skills.
- Ability to think independently.
- Flexibility, adaptability, resilience, and intuition.

The best employers go beyond the threshold skills, and evaluate the following:

- Does he show vision—seeing the possibilities (big picture), how all the parts relate to one another?
- Does she have intuition—the ability to make a leap of faith to go beyond the data to make a smart guess?
- Can he set a clear, compelling direction?
- Does she volunteer for projects and seek better ways of doing things?
- Does he view obstacles as mere roadblocks that can be overcome?
- Does she take the risk of personally leading a change project?

In the last chapter we saw how Steve dealt with Rhea's concerns. In this career profile, we'll see how Katherine, through great presentation, is able to convince Marshall that she is the best candidate for his consulting firm. What questions do you anticipate about your ability to perform successfully?

Career Profile: Job Competence
Know Your Value

Marshall interviewed Katherine for a position in his consulting firm that specializes in the non-profit industry. She knew he would challenge her on her "alternate" route to consulting. He asked her to give him her short career history.

Katherine began, "After graduating Brown University with a degree in Visual Arts and Anthropology, I decided to explore a few career possibilities. I worked for a year at Sotheby's in London as an Associate in the modern art department and volunteered in an art gallery. At the end of that time, I decided I would not pursue a career in art although I love the creative part of who I am. When I came back to the States, I landed a position as an Assistant Producer at a small cable television station, but it was too small to actually need me, so the job only lasted a year.

"A friend then recommended me to a private school whose mission is to provide an outstanding education to inner city children. I was hired to create, and then implement, an art program for the 300 students in grades K-8. I accomplished the task and, during the process, learned that I loved creating the program, but not teaching it. Since I loved the school, the mission and the people, I requested and received a transfer to the development office, which was an excellent fit. By the second year, I was supervising a small staff."

Marshall asked Katherine why she enjoyed fund raising.

Katherine answered "As I gained experience, I was able to crystallize my likes and dislikes. I love taking a problem that involves people, figuring out what needs to be done, and doing it with minimal supervision. I also enjoy leading people, as well as projects."

Marshall asked Katherine, "Would you talk about one of your work related accomplishments that you're proud of?"

Katherine said, "I was asked to attend a social function with the Director of the School and a major potential client who headed one of the 15 largest corporate giving departments in the country. At the last minute, the Director had an emergency and asked me to cover for him. I went alone, and found that the potential client and I had a lot to talk about. He asked penetrating questions about the mission, vision, and values of the school which I think I answered well."

"At the end of the conversation, I asked him if he thought we were worthy of consideration for donor dollars. He said we would definitely be considered, but, since it was October, we would probably have to wait until next year. We remained in touch. I invited him to the school for a visit which went well. In December, I received a call from him letting me know that he had some disposable dollars, and he was going to give them to us. Since that time, he has become one of the school's top donors."

"That's a great example. As you know, we have a number of applicants for a position in our firm, and I'm wondering why you think we should hire you."

Katherine never blinked. "I know that, with my academic background in the arts, I'm not your normal candidate. However, I have taken a number of courses in micro-economics, spreadsheet design, financial accounting, and statistics on my own time, and I have very good computer skills, so I feel that I have enough of the needed analytics. I also know that consultants often come to a firm without client, or buy side experience, and with a very analytical approach to problems. I feel that my industry experience and creative background will give me a different perspective on problems, and will provide your firm with a view of the world that may be unique. I also know that consulting is moving more toward coming up with a solution and helping the client to implement it, and I know the personality and motivators of the clients in a not-for-profit firm."

Marshall looked at Katherine and said, "That is an amazingly mature and well thought-out answer for someone at your level."

Although it took a whole series of interviews, Katherine won the job.

Results Orientation and Execution

Possible Interview Question: Tell me about a time you took a problem with an operational component from start to finish.

The most effective company presidents and CEOs tell us they recruit people who want to win, are used to winning, and talk easily about the thrill of winning. A CEO will often say he asks the candidate an open-ended question and specifically doesn't ask about the result in order to see whether the candidate talks about what he/she accomplished.

Being results oriented is having the ability to set measurable goals, agreeing to timeframes, and then holding each person on the team responsible for meeting those timelines. Then, if the goals are not met, it becomes the responsibility of the team to give assistance to others to help get the group back on track. In this way, each person is an independent contributor part of the time and a team member ready to assist others the rest of the time.

The interviewer will evaluate you on the following:
- Does she live to win?
- Is he thrilled about winning?
- Has she produced consistently over time?
- Does he insist on working in a performance-based culture?
- Is she a self-starter who takes ownership, responsibility, and accountability?

- Does he develop a solid strategy, with a tight operations plan and specific goals?
- Is she able to overcome obstacles?
- Does he show resilience (ability to function at maximum efficiency under adversity?)
- Does she show a driving interest in successfully achieving the company's product or service goals?

In the last chapter we saw how Janet, an ICU nurse, was able to demonstrate a bottom-line, results orientation. In this career profile, we see how Nick, a Peace Corps volunteer, demonstrates a bottom-line results orientation. We specifically selected industries which you might not think of in terms of bottom-line results to demonstrate how some people think. What accomplishments (academic, professional, and personal) will you use as examples? What are the bottom-line results for those accomplishments?

Career Profile: Results Orientation and Execution
The New School

Nick's two year assignment in Guinea, Africa, for the Peace Corps was ending. It had been an amazing learning experience and created lifetime memories. He also knew that coming back to interview for a job in business to use his economics and political science degree would be challenging.

He was interviewing for a position in the corporate strategy department of a well-regarded multi-national firm. If successful, he knew there could be a line position in one of the firm's businesses in a few years. He was very excited by that prospect, but surmised, correctly, that he would be pressed for results in his Peace Corps position.

The question came a little sooner than Nick expected. Clearly, it was on the interviewer's mind because it was the first question Mr. Lorenzo asked. "Please tell me about a Peace Corps project you took from start to finish."

Nick knew he needed to handle the question well AND give bottom line results. "There were many potential projects that needed attention, but the most pressing was the need for a community school for the children," Nick began. "We were in one of the most rural areas of the country, and I knew resources and supplies would be difficult to attain. But, before worrying about supplies, I had to go before the elders and convince them of the need—that the 97 children in grades K-8 should not all be educated in a single room with two teachers. I wanted to say 'could not' be educated, but that is what they had been doing for some time, and I didn't want to be disrespectful. By the end of the third month, I had built enough trust for the elders to entertain my idea. It took another month to persuade the elders we needed a common area and five classrooms in 3000 square feet.

"What did you do next?"

Nick continued, "Unfortunately, the rainy season hit, so we used the time for planning rather than building. I drew the plans, recruited one skilled building expert on loan from the Peace Corps in another part of the country, and convinced a few of the most skilled men in the village to join me. We obtained some scarce resources, and by the time the rainy season ended, we were ready to go. We recruited older students to help so they would be invested in the project. The additional planning time enabled us to complete the task in two and one-half months instead of the three months we had budgeted."

Mr. Lorenzo asked, "Was building the school the most difficult part?" Nick laughed. "That was the easiest part; convincing the elders was hard, but, by far, recruiting capable teachers was the toughest part, and is still ongoing. After the initial group of hires, I was able to recruit one additional teacher who had been trained in literacy skills, and so the two of us divided the students by their reading abilities into three groups. The research shows that, with ability grouping, reading scores can be improved dramatically in limited time. We were proud of our results—the average growth was to double reading comprehension in just nine months. We know that type of growth can't continue indefinitely, but it will continue above average for a few years, and it will dramatically improve the student's long-term prospects.

Mr. Lorenzo told Nick he had done a good job of quantifying how the project benefited the students. He also told Nick the quality of the example he chose was outstanding. Nick ultimately won a position in the department.

Fit: ability to forge relationships and work as a member of a team

Possible Interview Question: Give me an example of the ideal work culture for you.

Fit refers to your ability and willingness to become a productive member of a team. This takes self-management, self-confidence, and comfort with yourself. It also means having the interpersonal skills, especially listening and communicating, to relate to the members of your potential team.

The interviewer will evaluate you on the following:
- Does she have strong communication skills and the ability to present?
- Is he authentic, showing genuine regard for others?
- Does she have the presence to command respect throughout the company and with clients?
- Is he interested in helping others on the team?
- Does she enjoy working on a team?
- Is he self-confident with humility?
- Is she collaborative, and does she speak of trust and pride in working on her team?
- Can he be the leader of the team when called upon?
- Is she focused more on the organization's goals than on her own goals?
- Can he listen extremely well?
- Does she demonstrate empathy?
- Is he client-centered, and willing to go the extra distance for the client?

In the last chapter, we saw how John was astute enough to see that Erica did not want to be a corporate attorney. In this career profile, we'll see how Josh learned, in his short career, what drives and motivates him. He discovered that he was willing to accept the risk/reward formula of a commission-based salesman. How will you answer questions regarding your ability to fit into a team and organization?

Career Profile: Fit
Drive to Succeed

Elizabeth, the interviewer, didn't wait too long to ask Josh a question that always gave her data about someone's ability to fit the culture of her company. She said, "I know you're moving back to Colorado because you and your fiancée want to live close to her parents. Would you give me an example of what you think is an ideal company culture for you."

"Telling you how I landed my first, and only, job is a good way for me to answer the question," said Josh. "Halfway through my senior year, I began interviewing with two computer software companies. One had a better reputation; the other one was in the process of establishing itself, but seemed to be on the verge of 'making it.' The company with the better reputation was considering me for two positions, one in its entrepreneurial sales division, and the other in its corporate marketing and account management division. This company clearly had the inside track because of its reputation and the ability to sell its established product line. As I learned later, two strong managers, one in sales and one in marketing, each wanted to hire me."

"The marketing manager had a little more leverage than the sales manager, and the decision was made to offer me a marketing position. As far as the organization was concerned, my decision would be easy—great company, great reputation, and great career path. The only problem was that no one had probed for my needs or wants.

I was disappointed with the offer because I understood my own motivators and drivers. It was important to me to do well financially, so the sales job would be a better fit. I didn't know, nor would I have cared, that it was internal politics that resulted in the marketing offer, rather than the sales offer.

"Suddenly, the sales job at the second firm with heavy emphasis on commission income started to sound a lot better. I had a series of meetings with both sales people and sales management. There were some minuses, such as the number of quality products, but I was assured that would change in the near future.

"Basically, the job was a sales position with a defined territory that would be mine alone. The salary structure included a base salary, and a generous commission structure above a certain sales volume. I was certain that I could reach the targeted sales volume very quickly and move in the commission structure. I accepted the offer with great enthusiasm."

Elizabeth asked, "Was that the right decision for you?"

"Absolutely," Josh responded. "I was successful in sales from the start, I loved it, and I became a valued member of the team. Within a short time, I was asked to mentor some of the more experienced salesmen and saleswomen who were not as successful as I was."

"That's great," said Elizabeth. "What did you learn from the experience?"

Josh replied, "The lesson I learned was that it is my responsibility to manage my own career. The company has the right to select the best person and I have the right to select the job that will help me to realize my career goals." Shortly thereafter, Josh received an offer to be a commission salesman on the road to becoming a sales manager.

Passion: deep, heartfelt, authentic excitement about work and life that includes the ability to energize others

Possible Interview Question: Give me evidence, through a specific example, where you exhibited passion.

We simply cannot say this enough about passion: It is the tiebreaker. **IT IS THE TIE BREAKER.** If two candidates are regarded as equal, or almost equal, the one who will win the job is the one who demonstrates more passion. We are not talking about play-acting; rather, a real sparkle in the eye and enthusiasm for the work and the company. The interviewer will once again evaluate you, based on the stories you tell to support your competencies and to see how they relate to the company's mission and goals.

The interviewer will evaluate you on the following:
- Do his accomplishments show fire, desire, and strength of conviction?
- Does she exude optimism, excitement, emotional connection, and determination?
- Does he energize (or exhaust) others?
- Does she relish change?
- Does he have an intuitive sense about overcoming resistance to the status quo?
- Does she volunteer for projects, and seek new and better ways of doing things?

- Does he view obstacles as mere roadblocks to be overcome?
- Does she demonstrate imagination and creativity?
- Does he seek ways for people to be challenged and have fun?

In the last chapter we followed Jeff's path to Olympic Gold. In this career profile, Brad gives great evidence of the passion he brings to whatever he does. How will you give evidence of your passion for life and work?

Career Profile: Passion
NCAAs

Brad was told by classmates to be ready for a question about passion in his interview. He knew that to work in a technology services firm, one had to show passion for the work and the ability to work long hours with huge energy.

Sure enough, the interviewer asked, "Tell me about a time when you really wanted something, but it proved extremely difficult to get."

Brad said, "It isn't hard to think of one. It just happened near the end of college. I received a 'C' on my economics paper due to a misunderstanding as to the exact nature of the assignment. My immediate reaction was anger, as I thought about how hard I worked and how unfair the grade. Once I calmed down, I went to the professor and presented my case. The professor was mostly unrelenting, but he acknowledged one point. He said, 'Look, you actually turned your paper in ahead of the deadline, and I have given a small group of students a four day extension. If you want, you can re-write the paper and I will accept it as your original with no penalty."

"Under normal circumstances, that would have been a great offer, but not now. I thought better than to let the professor know my lacrosse team had just reached the semi-finals of the NCAA tournament, and the next four days were final preparations for and the final weekend of the tournament in Baltimore.

"On my way back to the dorm, I did a quick assessment. I was passionate about lacrosse and wanted a national championship, but I was also passionate about getting the best possible job in technology services. I knew that if I let the grade from the paper stand, I could be questioned about the lower grade during my interviews. In addition, pride was a major factor in my wanting the highest grade point average I could attain. By the time I reached the dorm I knew what I had to do.

"The next four days were among the most stressful of my life. Each day, I had a ramped-up practice on the field and, then, another two hour meeting for scouting reports and game preparation off the field.

"Immediately following lacrosse, I practically ran back to my room to work on the economics paper. The two days prior to leaving for Baltimore, I went to sleep at 4 a.m. I worked on the paper on the bus ride to Baltimore.

"Over the weekend, I was able to complete the paper and e-mail it to the professor by the Sunday night deadline. Simultaneously, my team was able to finish second in the Nation in lacrosse. I received an 'A' on the paper, which helped me to maintain my grade point average."

The interviewer determined that Brad's answer was one of the best answers he had ever heard. That exchange won Brad a spot in the company.

Summary

The wise candidate will prepare for the areas of most interest to the interviewer.
They are:
- Threshold Competencies.
- The "Normalcy" Test.
- Character.
- Job Competence.
- Results Orientation & Execution.
- Fit.
- Passion.

The specific skills in the job competence section that employers look for in young professionals are:
- Relationship skills & teamwork.
- Communication skills.

- Problem solving abilities.
- Drive to succeed.
- Client-centeredness.
- Analytical & computer skills.
- Ability to think independently.
- Flexibility, adaptability, resilience, and intuition.

Job competence, including threshold competencies, and character are the two areas for the most focus. Your content PREPARATION will give you the self-confidence in your ability to answer questions, so you can concentrate on building the relationship with the interviewer, and demonstrating your character. This is evidence of your PRESENCE. One aspect of your preparation is to assess your strengths, and what could be perceived as weaknesses, in each area. Extra preparation on perceived weaknesses will pay huge dividends during your PRESENTATION. Finally, if two candidates are equal, or almost equal, the decision will come down to who has the most PASSION for the job and the company.

STEP 10: Final Preparation and The Two-Minute Drill

On the day of the interview your physical fitness routine should be less than a full workout. The idea is to have enough exercise to remove some anxiety yet not so much that you tire yourself out. Usually 60-75% of your normal routine will accomplish the goal.

Interview Tip! Physical Exercise
Exercising on the day of the interview enables you to relax and gives you a chance to focus. Exercise 60 to 75 percent of a normal workout.

Your dress needs to be conservative for the industry and company. It is always better to hear you are overdressed than to look around and feel embarrassed because you are underdressed.

You will want to have all necessary information for the interview, including 10 printed résumés, prepared ahead of time. Finally, be sure to leave plenty of time and make sure you arrive early.

Two minutes before the interview, often while you are waiting in a reception area, is a great time for a final review. This includes what makes you unique, competencies and accomplishments, and the 60-second rule.

After we examine the "Day of the Interview" and "The Two-Minute Drill," we will discuss some case studies that illustrate the points.

The Day of the Interview

Physical Fitness
- Increases energy and stamina.
- Enables you to listen and respond in a clear, straightforward manner.
- Allows you to demonstrate energy and drive.
- Reduces stress.

Dress
- Conservative for the industry and company.
- The outfit you feel makes you most confident and comfortable.

Necessary materials
- Have 10 résumés printed.
- Writing samples (if required.)
- Any other material required.

Leave Plenty of Time and Arrive Early
- Have the directions and check them out in advance.
- Leave extra time for the trip.

Interview Tip! Scheduling

Leave plenty of time at both ends of the interview so that you arrive early and can remain late. This reduces stress and shows interest.

The Two Minute Drill

Psychology
- Be prepared with an intelligent, organized game plan.
- Show an overwhelmingly positive attitude.
- Say nothing bad about anyone.
- Don't volunteer negatives about yourself.
- Review examples that show accomplishments and perseverance.
- Present yourself with self-confidence and humility.
- Let your passion show; if you really want the job, ask for it.

Respect
- Focus on the interviewer-put other things aside.
- Greet the interviewer with a warm smile and a firm handshake.
- Make eye contact throughout the interview.
- Be prepared to discuss potential rapport builders or icebreakers in case the interviewer is distracted.
- Don't cut rapport building short. The interviewer will eventually move on.
- Help the interviewer create an exciting, stimulating, interactive conversation.

Uniqueness, Competencies and Accomplishments
- What is your unique selling proposition or "What makes you different?"
- Define 3-4 key competencies.

- List 5 accomplishments to defend each competency-must include how it impacted the bottom line.
- Be prepared for questions about "outside of work" activities-interests, drivers, and motivators.

60 Second Rule
- The interviewer has a limited attention span.
- Keep your answers short and on point.

Career Profile: Physical Fitness
Energy and Fitness

Rick was athletic and knew he was in excellent shape. He was surprised, however, that, in each of his eight interviews, he had been asked about his four years of college soccer and the fitness involved in the program. There was a lot of interest in the fact that he had been recruited as part of a group of six men whom the new coach hoped would turn the program around. The college had suffered through a number of years of losing seasons.

Rick told the interviewers, with some pride, that his team was 8-8 the first year and then the program took off. They won the league championship, and reached the quarterfinals of the NCAA Division I championships their junior and senior years.

When Rick met Calvin at the end of the second day of interviewing, Calvin had a few more questions. Calvin asked Rick to describe what an average day was like at school.

Rick told Calvin he would be up before class to do his weight lifting, spend the day in class, followed by two hours at practice, dinner, and studying. Calvin also asked about fitness in preparation for the following season.

Rick responded, "For each player, Coach established an individual plan that was expected to be accomplished over the summer. He indicated the expected increase in each of the various exercises in weight training. In addition, all of us knew that we would have the Cooper test on the first day back in the fall. That involved a two-mile run followed by a one-minute rest and another mile that had to be accomplished in 17.5 minutes. In order to pass that test, you had to run combinations of sprints, middle distances, and long distances every day in the summer. If you didn't pass the Cooper, you weren't on the team."

Calvin thanked Rick for coming in, and indicated they'd like him to come back for one more round of interviews the following morning at 8:00. The next morning, Calvin started Rick on a series of six interviews plus a lunch with yet another group of associates. The day ended at 6:30 p.m. Throughout the interviews, there were many more questions about Rick's fitness training and interests.

At the end of the day, Rick saw Calvin again. This time he didn't hold back. Rick asked, "Calvin, why has there been so much interest in my college soccer experience and fitness program?"

Calvin responded, "Rick, we know that you are smart enough to work with us. We have checked you out academically in every way possible. But you have no idea what it takes to be successful here. We have had many very smart people come here with great expectations and quit within six months to a year."

"Why?" Rick asked.

Calvin went on, "Energy and fitness are critical in our business. As you know, we work under great pressure. When we are interested in buying or selling one of the companies in our inventory, there is usually a very tight time frame. The deal will be done either quickly, or not at all. Sometimes you'll be working seven days a week for extremely long days, often 18 hours at a time. On occasion, you'll need to work with your team straight through the night to make a deadline. This rigorous pace could go on for a number of weeks. The regimen you followed for four years of college soccer is way beyond what most people would be able or willing to do. We have found that success in college athletics has a high correlation with success at our company. Almost everyone here competed in college sports."

Calvin went on, "One thing I forgot to mention. We will often fly home from halfway around the world on a Sunday, and need to be back in the office on Monday. Each person has his or her own way of adjusting to jet lag, but a number of us have determined that the fastest way to shake the time adjustment is to take a 10 mile run. We often do it together."

"There is another consideration that is incredibly important to us: teamwork. We are very apolitical in this company. We are focused on determining and reaching our goals and not on internal politics. We are also very thinly staffed. Consequently, having each person pull his or her own weight is critical. We are literally right next to one another in cramped quarters for hours at a time, and we require cooperation and good humor in working together. It's probably obvious that we need to love our work. Do you understand now why we spent so much time on your college athletics and fitness?"

Rick was silent for what seemed like a long time. Then he responded, "I see what you mean. This is a huge commitment, but I'm willing to make it. If I'm offered a position, I think I'll do a great job." Calvin responded, "I think you will, too." Shortly thereafter, Rick was offered a position and accepted it with full knowledge of the expectations and the rewards involved.

Career Profile: Dress
The Critical Decision

Candice agonized over her decision of what to wear to the interview. She spent hours online and in the department stores looking for the right outfit. A candidate for a designer position in an apparel company would be evaluated on what she wore. In addition, she knew she needed to wear the clothes of the apparel manufacturer where she was interviewing. She consulted with two of her friends who were the same age and had excellent taste. Together, they decided Candice shouldn't wear designer clothes because it was too far above what Candice could afford or be expected to wear (the "Normalcy" test.)

The three women ultimately decided that something from the "bridge" line of the company would be appropriate, more expensive than a candidate would be expected to wear, but not outrageously priced. The choice would show Candice's appreciation of fine clothes and her good taste. They also agreed that jewelry and makeup would be on the conservative side.

When Candice went to the interview, she felt confident. It was only a few minutes before the interviewer made reference to the great outfit Candice had on. Both knew she was wearing the manufacturer's clothing line.

All of Candice's stress over what to wear was rewarded a few weeks later when she was called into the head designer's office. She offered Candice the job, and during the conversation, she told Candice that she and one other candidate were the most highly qualified and very close in terms of background and skills.

The decision hinged, however, on the evaluation of dress as a representation of the skills that Candice would bring to the company. "Your outfit was perfect for the interview and it won you the job," the interviewer told her.

Interview Tip! Dress

Your dress should be appropriate and on the conservative side for the company (and industry).

Career Profile: Necessary Materials
Opening Jitters

Shari had been the top student in the sciences program at the University of Wisconsin, and was being recruited by a number of pharmaceutical companies for their R & D divisions. Shari had narrowed the search to three of the best-known organizations. She performed well in her first round of interviews, and now she was looking forward to the next round, which included her potential boss and other senior managers.

Shari's potential boss, Todd, wasn't looking forward to the interview that day. It had nothing to do with Shari. He had been traveling for the last three days and for 14 of the last 20 business days. That much travel was unusual for him, and heightened his immediate problem. He had a major presentation that had to be written, proofed, and practiced that day for delivery the next.

Todd knew that hiring a new research scientist was high on the list of priorities, but not today.

Shari knew her strengths included outstanding intellect, technical skills, and an intense desire to improve the human condition. She also knew she was often uncomfortable meeting people for the first time and engaging in informal conversation or chitchat. As much as she tried to overcome this challenge, she found it difficult. In some encounters, when the conversation was awkward, she became tense or flustered.

Todd wanted to take a few minutes to prepare for the interview with Shari, but it never happened. Todd pried himself loose from working on the presentation when Shari was waiting outside his office. Todd was somewhat comforted by the fact that he had enough experience, and was facile enough to carry off any interview. He was sure this one would prove no exception.

Todd invited Shari into his office and offered her a seat. He would normally have been willing to spend 10 to 15 minutes helping Shari relax and become comfortable in the interview setting. Perhaps due to his own pressures, he found himself struggling with conversation topics. Suddenly, he remembered Shari's résumé had a personal section that listed her interests and activities.

He excused himself and went behind his desk to look for her résumé. Todd became more embarrassed as he fumbled through the papers, but could not locate the résumé. Red-faced and uncomfortable, he finally asked Shari if she had an additional copy of her résumé. He defended his actions by mentioning that he had just arrived home from a business trip.

Shari was doing her best to remain calm during this part of the interview, but this was the toughest time for her under the best of circumstances. Now she was put on the spot, and had to produce a résumé. She had not anticipated this request and wasn't even sure she had a copy of her résumé. The longer she fumbled in her bag, the more uncomfortable she became. An observer watching the two people could have seen the humor in the situation, but neither Todd nor Shari saw anything funny about what was happening. In the end, neither of them found a copy of the résumé.

Todd had no choice but to come back to the interview setting and attempt to resurrect the strained conversation. Now he had a real problem in that Shari had subconsciously retracted to a level deeper within herself during the period of confusion. Todd had to work very hard to draw Shari out; he tried hard and she tried hard, but it never worked. She couldn't help but think how ridiculous it was that she didn't have a résumé, and he was thinking about why he couldn't find her résumé. When the interview ended, both people were relieved that it was over, yet were uncomfortable with their behavior.

Later that day, Todd called Shari to apologize for his lack of preparation. He asked her if there was any chance she would be willing to come in and see him again. She agreed, and when they got together, they had both laughed about their first meeting.

Fortunately, in this case, Shari had a great background and Todd was willing to accept responsibility for the poor interview. Ultimately, Shari received a job offer from Todd's company and accepted it. In another instance, not having a résumé might not have turned out as well.

Interview Tip! Professionalism

Have all pertinent materials and information, such as extra résumés and company research. Anticipate having to wait before you are interviewed.

Career Profile: Leave Plenty of Time and Arrive Early
The First Encounter

David knew he made a mistake the minute he left home. He was leaving 20 minutes later than he wanted due to a personal problem at home. The 20 minutes compounded his problem by throwing him into rush hour traffic. By the time he drove in the company gates, he was already 10 minutes late.

The first person David saw was Sam, a security guard. David was beside himself with the stress of the commute and the fact he was late. He got out of the car and literally sprinted over to Sam to get directions to the correct building. David was abrupt and to the point. Sam tried to be helpful, but his learning disability kept him from processing the request for information as quickly as David wanted and needed it. David was visibly disturbed, making Sam's task all the more difficult. Finally, David obtained the information and raced on.

David found Meredith, Mr. Aldrich's executive secretary. When he discovered Mr. Aldrich was running late and had not yet arrived, David's perception of the situation improved dramatically. He began to relax and got a grip on himself. While he chatted with Meredith, he discovered they both rooted for the same baseball team, and they had a great time predicting trades and second-guessing the manager.

By the time Mr. Aldrich arrived, David was relaxed and confident. They had a terrific meeting. There was strong rapport and David liked everything he heard about the organization—colleagues who care about one another- a company with mutual respect for everyone. David left the meeting feeling confident; Mr. Aldrich said he would be called back to meet other key players in the firm.

That night at the dinner table, Meredith told her family, who were also baseball fanatics, about the candidate she had met at work that day who knew so much about baseball. She described David so they could picture him. As she spoke, her brother Sam became more and more uncomfortable. He lowered his head. When Meredith noticed he had withdrawn from the conversation she asked, "Sam, are you okay?" He wouldn't speak for a few minutes.

When he said, "I don't like that man. He was mean to me. He scared me," Meredith was amazed. She questioned her brother, gathering all the details of his encounter with David. Meredith knew Sam liked everyone. Surely if he had such as strong reaction, there must have been something in David she had missed. Something worth thinking about.

When Meredith went to work the next day, she told Mr. Aldrich about her family's conversation, particularly Sam's reactions. He listened carefully and at the conclusion, restated to Meredith the importance he placed on interpersonal concern and caring within the firm.

David never received a call back. He waited a few weeks and started calling. Mr. Aldrich did not receive his calls. Finally, David called late one day and Mr. Aldrich answered the telephone. He was short and cold. "The job has been filled," he said.

As David hung up, he was stunned. His last meeting had been great. David never knew what hit him. He never dreamed that his encounter with the security guard was his undoing.

Interview Tip! Congenial Attitude

Treat every person you meet as if he were the CEO. He might have a direct connection to the CEO.

Career Profile: The Two-Minute Drill
The Unfair Interview

Laura was stunned. She had tried for months to network her way into the premier cosmetics company that was her first choice for employment. Every one of her attempts had been frustrated in one way or another, until, finally, she spoke with one of her neighbors at a block picnic. The neighbor had a great contact with the head of recruiting for the company, and he had enough leverage to help Laura establish a meeting. It happened very quickly and Laura didn't have an opportunity to do much specific research on the people she might meet.

Despite that, her industry-wide research had given her enough background to have an intelligent conversation, and she was not going to pass on her chance to have a meeting. Laura and Ann, the head of recruiting, really hit it off. Although they did not attend the same college, they had numerous friends in common, one of them a great friend to each of them. They also had at least one common interest, bicycling.

Ann was equally pleased with Laura's academic background and internships. Suddenly, Ann stopped and looked at her watch. Then she looked back at Laura and smiled. "Look," she said, "How much do you want to work here?"

Laura said, "A great deal. This is my number one choice."

Ann said, "This may not be totally fair, since you haven't had a chance to do all of your preparation, but you have enough industry knowledge. We are in the final stages of the first round of interviews for entry-level trainees. You are definitely competitive with our other candidates, and we will not be interviewing again for six to nine months. I can schedule you in for an interview but it would be right now. I am sure you'll do well, and you can do further preparation before your next round. What do you think?"

Laura said, "Wow, thank you very much. I definitely want to try. How much time do I have to prepare?"

Ann responded, "Probably five minutes. The interviews are just about over." Laura did her best to look in control, as she accepted.

Ann took Laura to the interview site, wished her well and left. Laura's first thoughts were to panic. Normally, she was a set a plan, do analysis and preparation, practice and arrive early kind of person. Here, she had only a few minutes to get ready.

Instinctively, she thought how she had been taught the "Two Minute" drill. She had notes about the company with her, so she took them out. As she went over the notes, she began to calm down. In terms of psychological preparation, she reminded herself how lucky she was to attain this interview, and the importance of positive attitude, self-confidence with humility, and passion for the work. She reminded herself that the interviewer was taking valuable time to meet with her, and she should help make the meeting interactive and stimulating. This would require focus on the interviewer's agenda, especially in an initial screening interview, and keeping her answers within 60 seconds and on point. She had prepared long and hard on her competencies and accomplishments, and had prepared a short statement on what she felt made her unique.

Suddenly, the interviewer appeared but Laura was ready. She got up and greeted the interviewer warmly with a smile and a firm handshake. She really was ready. Laura had a great interview, went on to the second round, and eventually landed the job.

Interview Tip! Flexibility

Being flexible is a huge benefit. It allows you to take advantage of a situation, say or do the right thing, without extra time to prepare.

Summary

The Day of the Interview
- Physical Fitness.
- Dress.
- Necessary Materials.
- Leave Plenty of Time and Arrive Early.

The Two-Minute Drill
- Psychology.
- Respect.
- Uniqueness, Competencies and Accomplishments.
- 60-Second Rule.

PART V

Presentation and Passion

Presentation/Execution: Ability to execute your game plan during the interview and to "close the sale."

- Assist in carrying the interactive conversation throughout the interview.
- Understand consultative behavior-determine the interviewer's needs and present your skills and abilities to satisfy them.
- Deliver your competencies, accomplishments, and uniqueness in a cogent, concise, and convincing manner.
- Give no answer longer in length than 60 seconds.
- See interviewer's challenging questions as an opportunity, rather than a daunting task.
- Convert the interviewer's mindset from "buy" to "sell."

Passion: Deep, heartfelt, authentic excitement about work and life that includes the ability to energize others.

- Demonstrate drive for excellence...love of the work...huge energy...the ability to energize, champion, motivate, invigorate, and inspire others.
- Show a relentless drive to initiate, execute, and accomplish goals.
- Present examples of your perseverance and determination-the will to achieve no matter how difficult the task.

- Drive to attain the company (as opposed to personal) goals.
- Speak and work from the heart-manifests as optimism, excitement, and emotional connection.
- Demonstrate a keen interest in the position, how the business operates, and how your role would contribute to realizing the company's goals.

Step 11: Interview Sequence

In "The Interviewer's Content Agenda," we mentioned that the interview, from the interviewer's perspective, consists of:
- Rapport building (building a partnership.)
- Professional content (the intelligence, skills and abilities to perform successfully.)
- Personal content (the personality/relationship skills to "fit" with the people.)
- Selling the candidate on the company.
- Closing the interview.

In this chapter, we'll present each phase of the interview in more detail. Then, in the next chapter, we will discuss human interaction and communication.

Rapport Building (Evidence of Presence)

Establishing rapport with the interviewer is critical for you. During the first moments of the interview, initial impressions are established. As much as interviewers are trained not to make snap judgments, suspending an opinion is difficult. How you dress, your physical appearance, the way you greet them, whether you smile and make eye contact, the firmness of your handshake, and your walk, all meld into that initial composite.

Interview Tip! Positive Comments
Speak only positively about everyone you know.

Once in the office, you and the interviewer will spend time getting to know one another. This also gives you a chance to become accustomed to the new environment. Candidates who are geared to the content part of the interview comment that this part of the interview is difficult because they want to get right to the "meat" of the interview. You must remind yourself that rapport building is critical. Forget content for now. If you establish a bond, then content becomes important. If you don't, you are mentally eliminated before you ever mention your skills.

The chances are that everyone who has been invited for an interview has the skills to do the job, and is probably in the same ability range. But are they all alike in terms of personal characteristics, attitudes, values, and style? No, they aren't. Most of the outstanding interviewers we have met say that, if they meet one candidate who is personable, and is head and shoulders above the rest of the candidates in terms of skills and abilities, it is no contest. They hire that individual. They are also quick to point out that, in most instances, it doesn't happen like that. With candidates in the same general range, it comes down to personal factors. And they will all tell you that "fit" is more important than skills at that point. The best technical candidate is often not the one to whom the offer is extended, because another candidate is deemed a better fit in the organization.

The key to effectiveness in this stage of the interview is to take your cues from the interviewer. If the interviewer seems to be relaxed, open, and comfortable with meeting someone new, then your job is easier. You become comfortable fairly fast, and it is easy for you to volunteer information about your past and present interests and activities. It becomes easy to keep an interesting and stimulating conversation going, even if you don't feel that you are naturally outgoing.

If, however, the interviewer appears neither comfortable with himself, nor the interviewing process, then your job is much tougher, but certainly not impossible. It may fall to you to keep the conversation going. Whether or not you have reached a comfort level is irrelevant because this is your one, and perhaps only, shot to meet that interviewer.

This is not as difficult as it sounds. Starting with a smile is tremendously disarming. Be prepared to converse in such a way that you are willing to give a little more detail to your answers (within 60 seconds.) Volunteer some personal information, such as where you grew up, your family background, or personal interests and activities. If you help the interviewer accomplish his task easily and effectively, you'll reap rewards.

Interview Tip! Initial Greeting

A warm smile and a firm handshake make a strong first impression.

Career Profile
Interpersonal Skills

Rebecca instinctively did the right thing. She had always been able to determine the most uncomfortable person in the room. Her friends were amazed by her ability to involve that person in conversation and help him feel comfortable. By the time she left the room, Rebecca had learned intimate details about the person that even close personal friends never knew.

After taking a year to travel, Rebecca was ready to enter the work force. She was concerned about her marketability due to her one-year absence, but she had not taken into account the tremendous interpersonal skills she had gained through her life experiences. She interviewed with three organizations and, before long, received two job offers.

Once in the position she chose, Rebecca was called into her new boss' office. Carol told Rebecca the interviewing team had been impressed with her interpersonal skills. Carol was curious; she wanted to know where Rebecca had learned such powerful techniques. Rebecca thanked Carol, and then laughed. "I haven't had any formal training. I come from a single parent family where I've had almost full time responsibilities with younger brothers and sister. I've had to learn to be both a good listener and persuasive. I've discovered that, if you ask a few open-ended questions and genuinely care about what the person has to say, almost everyone will open up."

Is it any wonder that Rebecca was hired?

If you can learn something about the interviewer's background prior to the interview, it can be a huge help. Clint never interviews without doing all the homework possible on personal background. Somewhere in the interviewer's history, Clint is sometimes able to find some common educational bond, mutual friends, and/or interest. This information often helps Clint cut through numerous layers of surface rapport to reach a deeper personal level.

This can help the interviewer both in rapport building and to reach a faster comfort level through association. The thought process is, "If Clint is Peter's friend (someone the interviewer knows,) then he must be okay." If Peter also happens to be bright, successful, hard working, and easy to get along with, then so much the better.

In terms of fit, this may translate to, "Peter is our kind of guy. So you may be our kind of person as well." You can see that even at this early stage of the interview, fit is important. And, as we have discussed, it remains very important throughout.

In some situations, however, you are not able to ascertain any information about the interviewer or other key individuals in the organization. This doesn't mean you will not be successful. It means you are probably in the same position as the other candidates, and you have to develop rapport during the initial conversation.

In summary, the candidate should go into this segment of an interview with one cardinal rule: **Do not cut the rapport building short.** You cannot control what the interviewer does, but you can control what you do. The key is to follow the interviewer's lead, while keeping in mind your own agenda (building rapport.)

This introductory phase of the interview helps to create an easy, conversational exchange. How do you know that the other person isn't a jogger, coach, or traveler just like you? If the two of you share the same interests, it makes for an interesting dialogue rather than a one-way monologue. So relax, smile, and go with the flow

.

Interview Tip! Rapport Building
Do not cut the rapport building short. It is a great opportunity for bonding. The interviewer will transition the interview to a business discussion when she is ready.

Transitions

Transitions can be subtle and hard to define in an interview, but they are important because you must be prepared to move with the interviewer. The great interviewer will help you with these transitions, but many interviewers will not. This first transition from *Rapport Building to Professional and Personal Content* is usually the easiest, and you will usually receive help. The interviewer might say, "It has been great to get to know you a little bit. Now I'd like to learn something about your business skills."

Professional Content (Your Ability to Present) and Personal Content (Your Opportunity to Demonstrate Passion)

The last two chapters have been concerned with professional and personal content. Professional content in an interview deals with your ability to perform the work successfully. The components of professional content are threshold competencies, job competence, results orientation, and execution.

The personal content section of an interview deals with your character, motivation, interest, drive, passion, and your ability to "fit" with your potential colleagues. While we have separated the topics to explain them clearly, an interviewer will meld them together in your interview. The portion of the interview which integrates your professional and personal competencies will be the most significant, and longest, part of your interview.

Transition

At the conclusion of this discussion in the interview, there is normally a transition from *Professional and Personal Content* to *Selling the Candidate on the Company*. This transition may be more difficult to determine, but it might begin with the interviewer asking you, "Do you have any questions?" or "I'd like to tell you something about the company."

Selling the Candidate on the Company

The interviewer's agenda, assuming that he thinks you are someone the company is interested in, is to sell you on the merits of the company. Normally, the interviewer will give you an opportunity to ask questions and make comments during this phase of the interview. Your agenda is *Testing the Strength of your Candidacy* and *Overcoming Interviewer Concerns*.

As a conversation progresses, the interviewer accumulates information about you. The better your preparation and fit, the higher the interviewer's comfort level will be. No matter how successful you are, however, the interviewer will likely have questions or concerns about your skills and abilities, relative to the specific job needs in one or more areas. The concerns may be caused by something that was (or was not) discussed. It may be caused by a word here or a phrase there. There may have been a misunderstanding of a question asked, an answer given, or of a nonverbal sign that left a little question.

Frankly, this is natural. Part of this relates to the fact that **seldom does any candidate fill the job specification 100 percent.** Another part relates to the role of the interviewer in the negatively oriented screening process. The very nature of the process seeks to find the things that are wrong so that another person can be screened out. You must be prepared to counter that thought process.

A concern in the mind of the interviewer is not fatal. It can often be corrected, sometimes easily, especially if it is a misunderstanding. What can be fatal is a concern that is not corrected by the end of the interview. It then becomes a damning statement if the interviewer thinks, "You know I really liked Susan; there was just one thing she said..." The need to deal with concerns, then, should be clear and obvious. Yet, the interviewer frequently does not introduce the subject, and the vast majority of job seekers won't touch this issue. Why not?

Dealing with concerns or potential weakness in any form is difficult under the best of circumstances. When the concerns deal with your skills, abilities, or personality, it is that much tougher. But we ask you to balance the difficulty of this task with the need to have the information out on the table where you can deal with it and resolve it. To us, it's no contest. Having the information is crucial.

The issue, then, becomes finding the best method to test this area while maintaining your comfort level and that of the interviewer. The best method is to request a comparison between the targeted professional and personal characteristics, and your own. You might ask:

"Mr. Jones, earlier I asked you to define the targeted professional and personal characteristics for this position. Now that you know a little more about me, can you compare my characteristics with the targeted ones?"

Or, "Mr. Jones, now that we have had an opportunity to talk about the position, I feel more confident than ever that I can be of assistance to your organization. Do you have any concerns about my ability to do the job or fit into the organization?"

Having asked the question, you must now be ready for the response and how to deal with it. You have asked a very direct question that requires an open, direct response. Some interviewers are able to deal with the question openly, and some have problems with it.

If you hear a vague response like, "Oh, I think your skills are fine" or "You certainly could do the job," you are probably not being given the information you requested. You might come back and say, "I appreciate those kind words. I am feeling good about the fit as well. What I was trying to do was to see if you had any concerns about my ability in any specific area so that I could address them while we're together." This again lays the issue right out there.

At this point, there is either a response and dialogue—or not. If you sense that the interviewer is not comfortable dealing with the issue directly, then you have no choice but to move on. However, take heart, because many interviewers are able to deal with this discussion more openly and honestly than you think. Remember that job seekers don't get these issues out on the table because they don't ask.

Let's suppose the interviewer is willing to deal with your question. The response to your question can be varied. At the positive end, the interviewer may say, "I'm feeling very good about your background and abilities. I am comfortable with what I've heard." You may want to come back to ask about concerns in specific areas, or if your intuition tells you the comments were genuine, you may accept them at face value. A response totally at the negative end is highly unlikely since the organization has spent time and money attempting to screen out individuals who do not have the technical skills required before they reach the interview process.

What you are most likely to hear is something in the middle that gives positive feedback yet raises a legitimate concern. Let's go back to the example of the candidate seeking a sales position. In response to the question about the ability to do the job, the interviewer might respond, "I am very comfortable with your responses to my questions. My concern lies in the fact that you don't have direct experience in sales."

Okay, a concern has been raised. Now your preparation gets the real test. The question in front of you demands a response, and you don't have a lot of time to prepare your response. Yet, obviously, this needs to be your best prepared and presented response. Since you've spent the time prior to the interview identifying strengths and weaknesses and preparing answers to potential weaknesses, you're ready. You say:

"Mr. Jones, I did say that I did not have direct sales experience in a consumer company, but I believe that my position as a senior representative which involved leading tours of the college and then staying in touch with potential recruits was, in fact, direct sales experience."

The conversation might continue as follows:
> **Interviewer:** What makes you feel that way?
> *Candidate:* If I just gave tours and had no ongoing responsibility for the recruiting effort, I don't think it would have been a sales position.
> **Interviewer:** Why was your involvement important?
> *Candidate:* Virtually all of the students had a number of schools they were considering. College research discovered that remaining

in touch with a potential recruit was the best way of having them select our college.

Interviewer: Give me a "for instance."

Candidate: I had a female student recently call me and tell me she had definitely decided to attend another college, but my persistence had given her doubts and as she thought about it more, she decided she would fit in better with the students at my college.

Interviewer: Did she sign up for your college?

Candidate: Yes sir, she did.

Interviewer: What do you think you do best?

Candidate: I believe I have the ability to build relationships with people and convince them I have their best interest in mind. I am also willing to address their concerns directly.

The conversation should continue for as long as the interviewer finds it is productive and until all of the concerns are raised and addressed.

Does this exchange guarantee that the interviewer's concerns are overcome? No. But it defines the concerns, gets them out in the open, and gives you the best shot at resolving them. In this example, you not only had a chance to resolve the interviewer's concerns, but also had an opportunity to reinforce a number of your skills and abilities. You may also have the opportunity to present additional skills that afford the opportunity to continue the business dialogue. This extends the time you are with the interviewer, which increases the probability of success.

Remember, you have another opportunity to overcome the interviewer's concerns in the thank you letter, which will be discussed later.

Interview Tip! Eye Contact

Make eye contact throughout the interview. This is particularly critical when being asked about potential concerns or weaknesses.

Transition

It is the interviewer's role to make the transition from *Selling the Candidate* to *Closing*. This transition is usually not hard to tell because the interviewer usually thanks you for coming in and may or may not volunteer what happens next.

Close

It is the interviewer's responsibility to close the meeting. What many job seekers forget or are reluctant to do, however, is to determine what happens next regarding their candidacy. Rather, there is a tendency to sit passively and wait until the company initiates contact. By employing the passive strategy, you lose the opportunity to understand what is happening.

Suppose, for example, you receive a job offer from another company with a defined time frame to let the organization know whether you accept. And suppose that this most recent interview is with the company where you have the greatest interest. It suddenly becomes critical for you to know when a decision will be made.

Let's go back and follow our sample interview through to a possible conclusion:

Interviewer: I've enjoyed meeting you and getting to learn about your background. I think I have all of the information I need. Thank you for coming in.

Candidate: I've enjoyed the time as well. I feel you are doing some really exciting things and I'd love to work here. Can you tell me how the process will progress from here?

Interviewer: Let's see. I believe that I'm the fourth person you've met. Is that correct?

Candidate: That's right.

Interviewer: There will be one more round of interviews with two of our sales managers.

Candidate: Can you tell me whether I'll be recommended for that round of interviews?

Interviewer: You are the last person I'm interviewing, and I'm impressed. You will be moving to the next round.

Candidate: Thank you. I'm excited about that. Can you tell me how many other candidates will be moving to the final round and when those interviews will occur?

Interviewer: There are three other candidates, and we are going to try to schedule them for next week.

Candidate: You mentioned two sales managers. Are there two positions open?

Interviewer: Yes, there are.

Candidate: Will the final decision be made soon?

Interviewer: Probably within three weeks.

> *Candidate:* Is there any additional information I should have to prepare for the interviews?
> **Interviewer:** I don't think so. Frankly, I'm surprised you have been able to obtain as much information as you have about the organization. That's impressive.
> *Candidate:* You were extremely helpful in my preparation and I wanted you to know how much I appreciate your help.
> **Interviewer:** You're welcome. You'll hear from me toward the end of next week.
> *Candidate:* Thanks for your time.

Do you know everything there is to know going forward? No, but you have learned some important information. You are going to the final round of interviews with three other candidates in about a week. There are two jobs open (which surprised you.) The final decision should be made in about three weeks. Furthermore, your efforts at preparation regarding the company and its people seem to have been successful. This is all excellent feedback and indicates you have handled yourself in a professional manner. You are also managing your job campaign because you know when and under what conditions the decision will be made.

A final point: By reaching the finals, you have successfully handled all aspects of the interviewing process that are within your control. From this point, personal chemistry and the interviewer's definition of fit are the determining factors unless one of the candidates "shoots himself in the foot." These things are out of your control. Your goal in the final round is to relax, be yourself, and interview the same way you have previously.

If you receive the offer, great. If you don't, then move forward confidently. Your interviewing technique is effective. The same personal and professional characteristics demonstrated in the next interview may help you secure the offer.

Interview Tip! Timeline
Ask the interviewer about a timeline for filling the position. Knowing that enables you to manage the timing of your job campaign effectively.

Summary

The best means of accomplishing your agenda is by approaching the interview as a sales call. Understanding interview sequence gives you confidence in what is coming next so you can concentrate on "the sell."

The sales call requires planning and involves:
- **Building rapport** (presence): establishing a partnership.
- **Professional content** (presentation): convincing the interviewer you have the skills to perform successfully.
- **Personal content** (passion): convincing the interviewer that you have the energy, motivation, and drive to perform, that you love the work, and that you will be an excellent "fit" with the people in the company.
- **Transitions**: having an awareness of when the interview is moving from one phase to another.
- **Testing the strength of your candidacy**: raising any concerns about your candidacy and overcoming those concerns.
- **Closing**: learning the next steps in the process and when they will occur.

Step 12: Win-Win Interaction

In the last chapter, we discussed the interview sequence. Now, we need to add some interaction to the mix. Interaction adds complexity because both agendas cannot be accomplished at the same time. Therefore, there has to be a give and take that allows the interviewer and you to accomplish both sets of objectives (the interviewer's objectives and your objectives) within a congenial, interactive atmosphere. Understanding this interaction and how it can help you to be successful is the subject of this chapter.

It's helpful to observe how a conversation might take place in a social setting, and then we can discuss the complexities added when a conversation is in an interview setting.

A Conversation
Suppose you are on an outdoor basketball court at your local gym, playing a game with three close friends. Suddenly, storm clouds appear, and within 10 minutes, the black sky is laced with streaks of lightning. At that point, everyone heads to the locker room and splits up. You decide to get an energy drink, and, at the bar, meet someone you don't know. You introduce yourself and start with small talk. It leads into a continuous conversation for 35 minutes. What key components would be necessary for you to spend that amount of time with a new acquaintance?

Did you pick some or all of the following?
- We established a rapport.
- We both clearly enjoyed the conversation.
- We found some topics that were stimulating and interesting to both of us.
- We both participated actively in an engaging conversation.
- We both talked approximately the same amount.

Clearly, one of the most important aspects of the conversation is participating actively in an engaging conversation. This is important in the job interview as well.

Successful interview behavior is all about presence (building a partnership,) presentation (executing your game plan,) and passion ("closing the sale.") Your goal is to do everything you can to help the interviewer create a stimulating and engaging interactive conversation.

Complexities in Job Interviewing

We have been discussing four concepts:
- Preparation.
- Presence.
- Presentation.
- Passion.

It's important to create specific, measurable goals for each of these concepts so you will be able to judge progress. We have discussed Preparation previously and the need to know 3-4 competencies with bottom line results, five accomplishments to illustrate each competency, and the development of a statement of your uniqueness. Let's identify specific objectives for Presence, Presentation, and Passion.

Objective 1: Presence- Build a partnership with the interviewer.
Did we discuss one or two common interests, acquaintances, or experiences? Building a partnership with the interviewer gives evidence that you will be able to build relationships with others in the organization.

Objective 2: Presentation-Accomplish the interviewer's agenda.
Did I present my 3-4 competencies and accomplishments clearly and concisely, and support them with bottom line results? The interviewer's agenda is to determine whether your skills, abilities, and personality fit the company's needs and environment.

Objective 3: Passion- Accomplish your agenda.
 Did I identify the organization's most critical needs and convince the interviewer that I have the energy, motivation, and drive, that I would love to work in this company, and I will be an excellent "fit" with the people in the company?

Achieving these three objectives is no small task, but there's more. It's complicated by the personality, style, and expectations of the interviewer, *none of which you can ignore.*

The interviewer:
- Is in a favored position.
- Controls the interview.
- Is the buyer.

It is important to examine these conventions because they dictate, to some degree, your behavior in the interview. The interviewer clearly is in a favored position because she has something you want—a job. As a candidate, you must be sure you assist the interviewer to accomplish her agenda, or you have no chance of being successful.

That the interviewer controls the interview is a time-honored convention. In virtually all interview training, the interviewer is taught that, once the rapport-building portion of the interview is completed, she should take control of the interview. This allows her to determine whether your professional skills and abilities and personal characteristics are an effective fit within the culture of the organization. This is accomplished, in most cases, by the interviewer asking short, open-ended questions that seek long, complete answers. When you complete an answer, the interviewer typically asks another question. This leads to a question/answer interview style. You must be aware of the control issue and understand that individual interviewers vary in their need for control. In any event, seeking a change in the communication pattern from question/answer to interactive dialogue is an important issue that requires sensitivity and finesse.

The interviewer is the buyer (and you are the seller.) Interviewing, from its early stages through the selection of the final few candidates, is a negatively oriented, screening out process. It's like a multilayer sieve that refines flour to its finest state. The interviewer doesn't want to spend time selling you on the merits of the company if there is no chance you will make it to the later stages of the interview process.

Consequently, the interviewer would rather spend time evaluating your ability to perform, "fit" issues, and your passion for the work. There is constant evaluation to determine where you stand in the priority ranking of candidates. You must understand this need as critical to the interviewer's agenda, and assist the interviewer to accomplish her goal. What is important to you is to do well enough in the interview to have the interviewer's "buy" become a "sell" as she decides that you will proceed in the interviewing process, or be offered a position.

Communications Flow

The key to your success in the interview is to become a partner with the interviewer in managing the communications flow, which is the percentage of talk by each participant. This task is complicated by the conventions we just discussed, including the interviewer's need to remain in control. Yet, a change from question/answer to an open, interactive dialogue is well worth the effort because it makes the interview more exciting, stimulating, and challenging for both you and the interviewer, and it dramatically increases your chances for success.

The best example we can give to illustrate the point is one that all of us have experienced. Think back to high school and identify your two or three best teachers (using any criteria you want.) Let's call all the other teachers in your high school the control group. Now let's focus on just one variable, the percentage of talk. First, decide whether the best teachers, on average, talked more or less in their classes than the control group teachers. Second, determine what percentage of time each group of teachers talked. When you have your answer, read on.

We'll bet your answer is that the best teachers talked less. Did you guess that the best teachers talked about 50 percent of the time, while the control group teachers talked 80 percent or more of the time? You were right.

Your outstanding teachers managed to have stimulating, challenging, classes that seemed to fly by because they involved you in interesting material and maintained a highly interactive conversation. Do you see the kind of climate we are trying to create in the interview?

Interview Framework

A simple framework can help you visualize communication flow during various phases of the interview. If you plot the pattern that most interviewers follow, then examine the pattern you would like to see, you'll be able to observe the similarities and disparities. When the agendas are the same, such as in the rapport building phase of the interview, you won't have to worry about conversation management. When there are disparities, such as in the content portion of the interview, you'll recognize what is happening and look for opportunities to improve your position.

The pattern most interviewers follow is to conduct initial rapport building with an interactive conversation with each of you talking about 50 percent of the time. When the interviewer makes the transition to the business portion of the interview (which we are calling professional and personal content) she likes to ask short, open-ended questions and have you talk 85-90 percent of the time. She is clearly a buyer at this time. If your answers satisfy her and hit the mark, she allows a gradual change to 50 percent talk each in the last third of the interview. This is, "selling the candidate on the company" and "closing the interview."

Interview Tip! Answering Questions

Answer the interviewer's questions directly/concisely. This gives the interviewer confidence that you are willing to help accomplish her agenda.

Figure 1 graphs the communication flow as the interview progresses from phase 1 (on the left,) which is the rapport-building phase, through phase 5 (on the right,) which is the close. The communications flow, which identifies the percentages of candidate and interviewer talk, is shown by line A.

The pattern you as the candidate want to follow starts with the same interactive rapport building (50 percent talk each) as the interviewer pattern. The difference comes in the content phases, where you would like to continue an interactive pattern throughout the interview. Since the interviewer is in control, however, it may not be possible, especially in the beginning of the interview, to reach an interactive conversation. Your role is to seek every opportunity possible to engage in authentic conversation, which makes it more like a partnership, than the standard question/answer format.

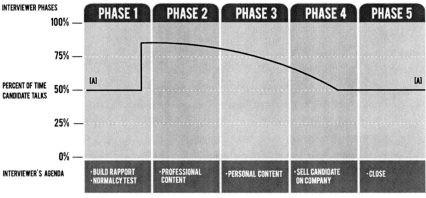

FIGURE 1. Communication flow: Ideal from interviewer's standpoint

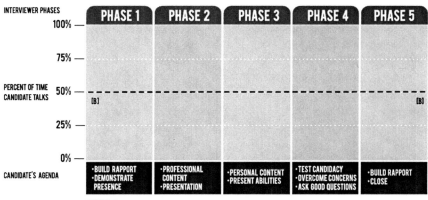

FIGURE 2. Communication flow: Ideal from candidate's standpoint

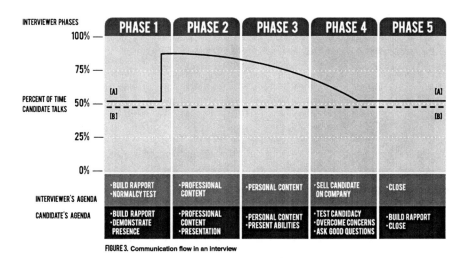

FIGURE 3. Communication flow in an interview

Interview Tip! Business Conversation
The goal is to create an exciting, stimulating 50-50 percent business conversation throughout the interview.

Figure 2 graphs the communication flow that you want throughout the interview, which is shown by line B.

Figure 3 merges the communication flow of the interviewer model (*Figure 1*) and the candidate model (*Figure 2*). The communication flow is shown by line A (the interviewer's model) and line B (the candidate's model.)

The interviewer and candidate's agendas are identified at the bottom of the graph.

It is clear that the agendas are parallel in phases 1, 4, and 5 and divergent in phases 2 and 3. The divergence represents the opportunity for the candidate and the interviewer to change the communications flow from a candidate-dominated pattern (talking 85-90 percent of the time) to one that approaches 50 percent talk each.

Parallel Phases in the Job Interview
In rapport building (phase1,) selling the candidate (phase 4,) and the close (phase 5,) there is a higher probability there will be an interactive conversation. This is what you are hoping for, so you will "go with the flow." That doesn't mean relax and forget that you are in an interview, but it does mean there is an interactive conversation.

Divergent Phases in the Job Interview
In professional content (phase 2,) and personal content (phase 3,) there is a greater probability that the interviewer will move to a question/answer style with short open ended questions seeking a long response (e.g."Tell me about yourself".)

In light of our discussion concerning how much more enjoyable interactive business discussions are for both interviewer and candidate, you should look for opportunities to change a less interesting monologue to a stimulating, interactive encounter. The change also makes the meeting easier for the interviewer because she doesn't have to take the lead all the time (by asking the next question or changing the direction.) Rather, the conversational ball can be passed back and forth like in a basketball game.

You will find great differences in interviewers on this point. If the interviewer willingly allows the communications to move away from question and answer toward a business conversation, then she is giving up some authority to dictate communications direction as well as change the communications flow (the percentage of talk by each person.) For one interviewer, this is a simple switch that makes a lot of sense. For another, it is a change of style that she might make only as she becomes comfortable with the candidate. For yet another, it is so alien to her personality and comfort level that it is an impossible change.

This poses two issues for you. First, you must be able to understand the interview sequence and anticipate what will probably happen next, so that you can respond appropriately. Second, you must be able to read whether the interviewer is willing to allow changes in the communications flow toward an interactive exchange.

Assuming the interviewer is willing to change to a business discussion (even for a brief period,) the percentage of candidate talk in the business portions of the interview (phases 2 and 3) is somewhere between the interviewer's model and the candidate's model. It is moving toward 50 percent talk by each participant and dramatically increases the chances for your success.

Career Profile
Business Opportunity

The notion that two participants in a conversation have different agendas certainly isn't new. It happens all the time in social settings. Suppose, for example, you are anticipating meeting Ed, a possible business contact. At a party after a concert, someone introduces you to Ed. After the introductions, he asks you what you thought of the performance. The focus of the conversation stays on the selection of the songs that were played and what each of you thinks of the group that performed. Soon, a friend of Ed's comes by, and Ed turns his attention to him. You're cordial and hide your disappointment. The moment is lost.

Clearly your agenda and Ed's were different. You would have loved for the conversation to turn to business, even in that first encounter. Ed's agenda, however, was purely social. Once the disappointment is gone, you realize that it was, in fact, a good encounter because you met Ed and can build on that. You realize it was probably unrealistic to talk business the first time you meet anyway.

Suppose you'd like to build the relationship. You do some homework about Ed's office supply business and find out he has increased the business by $5 million in the past four years. It is growing by leaps and bounds, and he is going to need additional staff, if he wants to take the business to the next plateau. You know that your experience working retail in the summers selling office supplies for one of the largest chain stores could be helpful.

At another party some months later, you are fortunate to catch him alone. After exchanging pleasantries, you remind him of your first meeting and then say, "I've been reading some wonderful things about your company. You must be excited about your rapid growth." He is genuinely appreciative of your comment and tells you about the business. Ed is amazed to learn how much you know. When he asks what you do, he is extremely interested in both your background and the industry knowledge you could give him. He suggests you get together for a business lunch with one of his managers so the firm can get to know you better, and you willingly accept. Three months, and a series of meetings later, you happily accept a job as the newest employee of Ed's company.

In these two brief encounters, we saw divergent and parallel agendas. Success depended on sizing up the situation and then having the patience to wait for the right moment. When that moment occurred, content and presentation became important considerations in the successful outcome.

Screening/Hiring Interviewers

We are often asked whether the interview framework is applicable to screening as well as to hiring interviews. The answer is that it applies to both. Some differences between the two types of interviewers are only minor variations on a theme, rather than a completely new one.

In the screening process, you are likely to interview with a recruiter or human resource (HR) professional. Their roles are to address professional content first and personal content second, and to screen out candidates so that the hiring manager has to deal with only a small pool of highly qualified applicants. High on their list are thoroughness, efficiency, and time management. Their preferred styles of interviewing are often to control the meeting by asking open ended questions having to do with your skills and background and then evaluating your answers (i.e., looking for reasons to eliminate you.)

The screening interviewer will usually spend less time on personal content. To the degree they do evaluate personal content, however, it will require dialogue, and dialogue affords you opportunities to accomplish your agenda as well. Still, keep in mind that, under normal circumstances, it will be more difficult for you to move the discussion toward a 50-50 percent business discussion with a screening interviewer than with a hiring interviewer. Your goal is to do the best you can.

The hiring interviewer is usually a line manager who is concerned with finding someone who can perform successfully in the job and who is an excellent fit with those in the department and the company. She may begin the interview in a question/answer manner, but often engages in a dialogue to find out about your professional and personal content. The reason for this is that she has a real business need to have a partner (or subordinate) to carry out the mission of the organization. She is less concerned with interviewing procedure than with finding the right person to assist her.

One great interviewer we know says that he asks herself, "If I were working long hours on an emergency project, is this someone I'd like to have working with me?" This point of view will make it easier to engage in a business dialogue, and that makes it much easier for you to accomplish your agenda. It also creates a more stimulating environment for both you and the interviewer.

Summary

The key components in creating a win-win approach to landing your ideal job are outstanding preparation, and also include:

- **Presence: Build rapport with the interviewer.** Did we discuss one or two common interests, acquaintances, or experiences? Building a partnership with the interviewer gives evidence that you will be able to build relationships with others in the organization.
- **Presentation: Accomplish the interviewer's agenda.** Did I present my 3-4 competencies and 5 accomplishments clearly and support them with bottom line results? The interviewer's agenda is to determine whether your skills, abilities, and personality fit the company's needs and environment.
- **Passion: Accomplish *your* agenda.** Did I identify the organization's most critical needs and convince the interviewer that I have the energy, motivation, and drive, that I would love to work in this company, and I will be an excellent "fit" with the people in the company.
- **Conversation: Establish an interactive, stimulating (50 percent talk each) conversation.** An interview is the most exciting, stimulating, and fun when it remains interactive from start to finish. The closer you get to 50-50 percent talk throughout all phases of the interview, the better both the interviewer and you feel about the interview.
- **Convert the interviewer's mindset from "buy" to "sell."** As you assist the interviewer to understand your skills/abilities and

personal characteristics, the interviewer becomes more and more comfortable with you. Eventually, the "buyer" (the interviewer as buyer) becomes a "seller" (the interviewer selling the merits of the company to you.)

- **Demonstrate your love of life and work, your energy, and your ability to energize others.** Everyone would rather work with someone who is positive, outgoing and enjoys life.

Step 13: Effective Interview Strategy and Tactics

The interview interaction showed where agendas were parallel and divergent. This chapter gives you suggestions for successful behavior in each of these interview phases. The importance of Preparation, Presence, Passion, and Presentation will be evident throughout the discussion.

We will follow the sequence established in the framework, moving from phase 1 to phase 5 of the interview. These headings follow the basic pattern of an interview, namely that the interviewer will spend time getting to know you prior to dealing with the interview content (professional and personal content.) Your own agenda, as has been mentioned throughout the book, has to come after your participation in the interview to help the interviewer achieve her goals. Then, you can work to determine company needs, and, finally, present your abilities as a match for those needs.

Assuming that you are deemed a good fit, the interviewer will sell you on the benefits of working for the company, and then close the interview. However, remember that, in the dynamics of the actual interview, there will probably be a good deal of jumping back and forth from one phase to another.

In phases of the interview where your agenda and the interviewer's are in sync, you stay focused and "go with the flow" (phases 1, 4, and 5.) In phases where your agendas differ, the use of interview strategy and tactics increase the chances for creating an interactive business conversation and bring better results (phase 2, and 3.)

Phase 1: Building Rapport

Interviewer's Agenda:
- Build rapport.
- Utilize the "Normalcy" Test.

Your Agenda as the Candidate:
- Build rapport.
- Establish your presence.

(Note: These headings correspond to the interviewer's agenda and to the candidate's agenda found in the previous chapter.)

Interview Tip! Relax

We're serious; relax! Approach the interview as an enjoyable opportunity.

The interviewer and candidate's objectives are more similar in the first phase than in any other phase of the interview. In most cases, the interviewer is more than happy to engage in an interactive conversation and is interested in building rapport, and conducting the normalcy test discussed earlier. Your agenda is building rapport and demonstrating your presence, the ability to form a partnership. An interactive conversation should be fine with you, because it affords an excellent opportunity for you to adjust to normal interview stress and the new surroundings. It is important to remember that these opening minutes are definitely part of the interview; your behavior is being evaluated through the quality of the conversation.

There is usually some small talk, as would happen if you met someone in a social situation. You might be asked, for example, if you had any trouble with the travel directions. (This is the only time in the interview that you might tell an untruth. Even if the directions took you from Chicago to Dallas via Miami, you say, "The directions were great." Remember that the interviewer or someone close to him gave you the best directions they could.)

Rapport building is a time of great opportunity (and risk) for you. In today's highly competitive marketplace, the best jobs draw a number of very well qualified candidates. As we have discussed, the difference between candidates often comes down to personal chemistry—not technical skills. The interviewer is trying to answer questions like, "Who is the best fit in my organization?" and, "Who am I most comfortable with?" Building great chemistry starts at the beginning of the interview.

Interview Tip! Bond

If the interviewer "falls in love" with you, great things can happen. You may be hired, for example. If rapport is not built, nothing good will happen.

Career Profile
Rapport Building

A greater percentage of jobs are won (and lost) in phase 1 than you might think. Colin had acquired a strong construction and operations background working on a number of projects in high school and college. Since his girlfriend was a year behind him in college, he decided to remain in the area. He searched for a position and identified a company that seemed exciting.

When he went to interview with the head of the operations area, he had normal interview apprehension. During the rapport building, the interviewer asked Colin about his outside interests. Colin said that he had been volunteering to work construction for an addition on a church in the area. The head of operations was surprised, and told Colin he was doing the same kind of project for a local non-profit organization. The one-hour interview lasted two and a half hours, and Colin was absolutely clear why he won the job.

The one thing you don't want to do during this time is to cut off the personal interaction. It almost seems like something that doesn't need to be said, but it does. A bright, assertive person sometimes comes to an interview ready to get down to business. If the interviewer makes small talk for too long, the candidate wants to grab him by the throat and shake him. No matter how bright and well qualified they are, these candidates are shortly on the "Don't call me, I'll call you" list. Relax. Enjoy the conversation. See if you can learn something about the interviewer. Let the interviewer begin to "fall in love" (in a business sense) with you. Maybe you'll discover some common interests, activities, or people. The chances of being offered a position are significantly higher if the interviewer thinks you're great and enjoys being with you.

Interview Tip! Build Rapport
Don't cut rapport building short. The interviewer does it soon enough.

Tactics:
- Ask yourself, "Does it look like I am enjoying myself?"
- Smile, laugh (when appropriate.)

- Be approachable and friendly.
- Help the interviewer keep the conversation moving.
- Discuss your interests (one may be a mutual interest.)
- Identify common experiences and/or friends.
- Show enthusiasm for the interviewer's interests.
- Be positive.
- Do not (EVER) cut off rapport building.

Phase 2: Professional Content—Can you perform successfully?

Interviewer's Agenda:
- Evaluate professional content.

Your Agenda:
- Present professional skills and abilities clearly and succinctly.
- Ascertain company needs and clarify them.

Whenever the interviewer feels it's time, he makes the transition to the business portion of the meeting. When this happens, he wants to learn about your professional background, including general intelligence, technical skills, and experience. The professional background check is to be sure you meet the company's job specifications.

Research concerning your background took place prior to the interview, but face-to-face discussion is also critical. If you are new to the job market, he will want to learn about your academic career and internships. If your have had job experience, he wants to understand why you accepted and left each position to gain clues to what drives and motivates you. Although your own agenda calls for you to learn about the company, the position, and the people, hold off for a while. **Follow the lead of the interviewer.** Although we are focusing on professional content, the interviewer will continue to evaluate your personal characteristics throughout the interview.

The style the interviewer selects is less important than your ability to recognize and react to what is happening. With this recognition, you are in a position to implement strategies that lend themselves to a win-win interview. Let's take the worst-case scenario and assume the interviewer stays glued to a question/answer format.

Perhaps the interviewer asks you three, four, or five open-ended questions about your background that require fairly long responses. Suppose the first question is, "Tell me about yourself," or "Why don't you tell me something about your education and career history?" If left unchecked, this pattern quickly adds up to 80 percent candidate talk with little interaction or information gained. An additional concern is that, with all the talk, you must maintain the interviewer's interest.

The best way to stay on track and keep interviewer interest high is to keep your answers short. This also helps to keep your percentage of talk from skyrocketing. (Note: Earlier we discussed the sales research indicating the importance of keeping your answer to 60 seconds.) Then, if the interviewer wants, you can go back and give greater detail on any part of your answer. This will help maintain his interest. In response to the question, "Tell me about yourself," the answer might be given as follows:

> **Candidate:** Well, I grew up about an hour outside of Oklahoma City. I have one brother who is younger than I am. My father sold industrial heating controls and my mother was a secretary. The love of my life while growing up was sports.
> *Interviewer:* That's interesting.
> **Candidate:** I was recruited to go to the University of Oklahoma where I was a general studies major and a starter on the basketball team. In my junior year, I also became interested in tornado tracking.
> *Interviewer:* Really?
> **Candidate**: Really. I was hired by a television station, taught to use a hand held camera and, together with two other students, sent out to do what others considered the dirty work of following tornados.
> *Interviewer*: It doesn't sound as if you think it was such bad work.
> **Candidate:** To get paid to go on an adventure? No, we thought it was great work.

Interview Tip! 60 Second Rule
You have 60 seconds to make your point or you will lose the interviewer.

When to Ask Your Question

As you answer a number of the interviewer's questions, a comfort level starts to develop. The interviewer gets to a point where he is at ease with the way things are happening in the meeting and with the answers you are giving (due to your outstanding preparation). You won't need anyone to tell you when the interviewer is comfortable with the conversation flow.

As the interviewer's comfort rises, windows of opportunity will begin to appear for you to do needs development. In a question and answer format, they usually occur at the end of one of your answers. You know when your answer is going to end. The interviewer doesn't. If you end your answer by completing your thoughts on the information requested, then you will be asked another question and the pattern continues. But suppose that, instead of merely ending your thought, you ask a question that directly relates to the discussion, one that seeks information about the interviewer's business needs. Let's look at an example.

> **Interviewer:** Was that your most defined work experience?
> *Candidate:* I would say, 'Yes,' because most of my summers were spent preparing for basketball season.
> **Interviewer:** Can you tell me about your duties in the tornado tracking position?
> *Candidate:* Yes, my duties consist of three major components. They are ...(elaborate on your duties) ... Can you tell me about some of the skills you are looking for?

Frankly, the candidate question can be worded in any number of ways. For example:

"Are any of my recent responsibilities similar to your needs?"
"Can you tell me something about the position you are filling?"
"Can you tell me about the objectives the successful candidate will have in the first few months?"

If your "read" is correct and the interviewer has reached a comfort level, he answers your question. During the brief time he is answering the question, you are obviously not talking, which slightly lowers your percentage of talk. However briefly, you have switched to a business discussion or conversation format. When you ask the question, however, there is a range of options available to the interviewer.

The worst thing that can happen is the interviewer doesn't like the fact you have asked a question and doesn't respond or indicates he would rather not answer a question at this time. Let's say the interviewer just went right on and asked another question. This is rare, but, if it happens, assume you made an incorrect read and flip back into your "answer the question" mode. Patience is critical with this interviewer. You then have to read the signals for a period of time before you try again. Even then, you may not feel very comfortable trying to ask a question because you were rejected the first time.

Given an opportunity to ask another question, you may be more comfortable if you explain why you need the information: "If you could define the department's key goals over the next year or two, it will help me to target my skills and abilities to those needs."

Another possibility is that the interviewer answers the question and then immediately reverts to the question/answer format. This is clearly moving in a positive direction. The fact that he responded expresses a willingness to give some information although his comfort level remains with the question and answer style. The behavior, however, leaves the door open for you to try again in a few minutes. (Note: We are not suggesting you ask a question after each question you are asked. Use judgment.)

A third possibility is that the interviewer is receptive to the question and provides an opportunity for dialogue. Then, after the topic is fully covered in a conversational format, the interviewer switches back to a question/answer mode. This option dramatically changes the percentage of talk (toward 50-50 percent) during the dialogue period and gives you an opportunity to raise questions and generate information.

Finally, the dream option is that the interviewer is receptive to your question, provides an opportunity for dialogue, and does not switch back to a question/answer format. This causes a total switch to a conversational format, changes the percentage of talk closer to 50 percent each, and provides an opportunity for you to be an equal partner (almost) in the conversation.

If the last two options seem to be a fantasy, they're really not. Remember that a business discussion or conversation is a much more relaxed and comfortable style for the interviewer as well as good for you, and the switch often makes the meeting more interesting and informative. Consequently, there is strong incentive to remain in a business discussion. Once in this mode, if the interviewer continues to feel that he is getting the information he needs, there may not be great incentive to change.

Career Profile
Changing Gears

As you become comfortable with the concept, you will find that you can encourage a switch in any number of ways. For example, Rick went back for a second interview with an automotive company. He knew that strategy meetings had been taking place during the three weeks since he had visited; his agenda was to learn about his potential boss's current thinking and how that would affect his previous discussions.

At the conclusion of the personal rapport portion of the interview, Janice began a question/answer format with Rick. After a few minutes of straight question and answer, Rick said, "You know, it has been about three weeks since we last met. I remember that you mentioned that your department was getting ready for strategy meetings and I wonder if you would tell me how they're going. It would help to bring me up to speed." The comment was perfect. It fit within the context of the discussion, and asked for help in understanding what was happening.

Janice answered the question in detail, and the discussion became an open dialogue. The meeting remained a discussion from that time forward. You will not always completely change a pattern, but you won't know what you can do until you try.

Seeking Clarification

Another technique for changing the communications flow and testing your focus is to ask for clarification. This works well when the interviewer is reluctant to change from question/answer to business discussion, or when you are not sure what information interests the interviewer. Suppose, for example, the interviewer asks, "What are some of your outstanding accomplishments?" This question is so broad that you have no idea what information might be of interest. The more direction you can get, the more you can focus your answer. You might proceed as follows: "Mr. Jones, is there a particular area of my background where you'd like me to focus?"

You might hear, "Anything you want to tell me," and, in that case, you take your best shot at giving your outstanding accomplishments as briefly as possible. Our experience, however, is that this does not happen as often as you might think. Executives are busy and many prefer to get to the heart of the matter. Consequently, you might hear, "Certainly, I'm most interested in your tornado tracking job," or "Tell me what you learned when you were playing Division I basketball."

Even this brief exchange has helped you in two ways. It has focused the conversation toward the interests of the interviewer, and it has slightly reduced your percentage of talk, moving the discussion closer to a business discussion.

As you begin to have success in changing the conversation flow, you're going to be looking for information about the company and people, in addition to specific information about the position. Your interest at this point is threefold:

1. You need to answer the interviewer's questions regarding your professional skills and abilities in a clear and concise manner.

2. You need to gain information about the company's needs before you can sell your skills and abilities. You would also like to learn how the interviewer sees the position being structured (to whom it reports, authority/resources, accountability,) the goals (six months, one year, three years,) and how the individual is evaluated (how is success defined.)

3. In addition, one of the best questions for future reference is, "Would you describe the ideal candidate for this position?" The answer to this question gives valuable information to assist you when it comes to testing your candidacy.

The Need to Listen and Listen and Listen...

To this point, we have been talking about what you might do to move the conversation toward a business discussion if the interviewer is in a question/answer style. The purpose of creating a stimulating, interactive conversation is that it is more interesting, and you have a better opportunity to learn about the needs of the organization. This, then, provides you maximum time to sell your skills and abilities to solve those needs.

Developing organizational or individual needs requires the ability to listen to the other person's business problems, and be able to restate them accurately. It requires listening skills, the ability to ask penetrating questions, and to synthesize the information given. Finally, the ability to show empathy and an authentic sense of concern are needed.

The hardest part of listening for many people is to resist the urge to start thinking about what to say next. You may have an impatient side that wants to jump in and speak before the other person has even finished a sentence or question. You feel that all you need is a thread of an idea. "Hold it, hold it," that impatient side says, "I can finish that thought. I can add value to the conversation." Active listening requires concentration and discipline. It's hard work, but it's an invaluable interview tool.

Interview Tip! Developing Needs

Ask what the interviewer's needs are and confirm that you
understand them.

Questioning and Assessing Needs

After listening (and listening and listening,) your questioning skills and
ability to uncover the needs become important. It normally takes a good
deal more concentrated questioning than one thinks to understand someone
else's needs. After all, you're coming to the discussion cold or with only
partial information, while the interviewer has been living with the needs
every day, and understands the problems and opportunities inside and out.

Problem solving skills can be particularly helpful at this time. Intelligent
candidates realize the interviewer is their greatest resource. It demonstrates
strength and intelligence to ask for help. For example, "Am I correct that
your real need is in hiring someone who will take an educated risk?" Once
the need is developed, you are able to confirm the needs.

In summary, the critical issue in this phase of the interview is that you have
to support the interviewer in establishing his style for the business portion
of the interview, and in accomplishing his agenda. You cannot have a successful interview unless the interviewer does. Once the interviewer gains
a comfort level and obtains the information that is important to him, then,
and only then, do windows of opportunity appear for you to pursue your
interests. Your agenda is to determine the needs of the organization, to confirm them, and to show how you can be productive. If, during the interaction, it is possible to change the conversation from question/answer to
business discussion, then the potential is the greatest for a stimulating,
enjoyable, and productive conversation for the interviewer and you.

Interview Tip! Consultation

Propose how you can help to solve the company's needs or
how the organization can use your skills.

Tactics
- Focus on the interviewer's needs first, and satisfy them.
- Learn the interviewer's preferred style (question/answer, business
  discussion, case study.)

- Adhere to the 60-second rule (no answer longer than 60 seconds.)
- Change the format from question/answer to business discussion. (Your objective is to talk 50 percent of the time.)
- If you're not sure you're on track, ask. For example, "Is this the type of information you had in mind?"
- Learn about the company, the position, the people, and the goals for the position.
- When the interviewer speaks, listen, listen, listen (this is the most important skill in relationship building.)
- Show that you are listening through eye contact, alert focused posture, and a quiet body.
- Learn the personal and professional characteristics of the ideal candidate.
- Be positive.

Phase 3: Personal Content including Fit

Interviewer's Agenda:
- Evaluate personal skills including fit.

Your Agenda:
- Demonstrate passion for life and work.
- Present abilities.

The interviewer's concern, in this phase, is with that nebulous quality called "fit." The interviewer is basically asking himself whether your personal style and approach will work well in the company. Fit was defined earlier as trying to determine a match between the ways the business is done (the environment, products, and services) and the values, integrity, and goals of the candidate (ability to function successfully as an individual and team contributor.) Interviewers begin to get a feel for fit in the rapport building at the beginning of the interview and continue throughout.

A primary way interviewers might approach fit is by asking you to address specific business situations you have faced in your business career. These are called behavior-based questions. They can have you describe a specific problem, your thought process in attacking the problem, the way you identified possible solutions, why the selected solution was chosen, the degree of success you attained, and, finally, what you learned (e.g. Tell me about a problem you resolved involving members of your team or organization.)

Interviewers are interested in how and why you made your decisions, and want to explore your thought process as fully as possible. It is important to allow them to pursue this line of questioning until they are satisfied, even if the amount of time on one topic seems endless to you. In fact, the better the interviewer, the longer he is able to remain on one topic.

Interview Tip! Problem Solving
Demonstrate flexibility in your approach to problem solving. You might say, "I would try X, gather data, and evaluate how it worked."

As the candidate, your interest during this part of the interview is in answering the behavior based questions and presenting the skills and abilities that convince the interviewer you are the best candidate (especially those on your teamwork, leadership, and ability to get things done.) The wise use of time in making your presentation is critical to an efficient sell. You have limited time to make your points, which increases the importance of outstanding preparation. Let's examine this issue more closely to understand the time constraints you are dealing with.

Let's assume you are successful in achieving your goal, and a 50-50 percent business conversation develops during the interview. Let's also assume an average interview length to be approximately an hour. Given that ten minutes are spent on rapport building and five minutes are spent on the close, approximately 45 minutes remain for the business portion of the meeting. Since only one-half of the 45 minutes might be yours, you are left with 20-25 minutes to ascertain information about the company, its goals, and its people, understand the needs, present your skills and abilities, raise concerns and resolve them, and be involved in the close.

However, that analysis makes a major assumption the interviewer doesn't need any of the time allotted to you to attain the information needed to make a decision about hiring you. Throughout the book, we have stated that interviewers are in a more favored status than the candidate; hence, the need to accomplish their agenda first. So, if interviewers need more time, they take it. Obviously, it is in your best interest to work with them.

Do these limitations seem a little overwhelming? They are if you are not completely prepared and cannot present things in a clear, crisp manner. Effective selling of your skills and abilities depends on three questions:
1. Have you discovered and confirmed the real needs of the organization?

2. Have you prepared by identifying your best accomplishments to illustrate your key skills and abilities, including bottom line results?
3. Have you practiced in order to present the skills and abilities in an honest, straightforward manner with a smooth, organized delivery?

With these factors in place, time constraints are not so intimidating.

Assertive candidates can employ another strategy in addition to using time wisely. It is preparing a proposal of fit. (This is our term; you call it anything you want.) This proposal helps the interviewer by analyzing how your skills can benefit the organization. The importance of the concept is that it is the candidate's responsibility to make this happen, not the interviewer's. Understanding where you might fit is a developmental process that becomes more complete as you learn more about the organization and meet more people.

On the first interview, you may know only what you have been able to learn from library and online research. During that interview, you learn more about the organization and where it is headed. As you move from the first interviewer to others (or to the same interviewer a second or third time), you may very possibly move forward during an interview, and then slip back to square one (in terms of progress in the interviewer's head) between interviews. In fact, this is likely to happen if there is time between the interviews, because the interviewer forgets about you shortly after you leave the office and he goes back to work. When you come back to see him (or another interviewer,) everyone has forgotten a lot about the last conversation, and you start over again.

As a business consultant who would like to complete a sale, your role is to analyze what you learned after an interview, and determine how you can assist the company to achieve its goals. Then, when you have another interview, you are able to update the interviewer concerning prior discussions and indicate how you can help. Whether this is a defined opening with a clear job specification, or a less clearly defined job creation, makes no difference. In the former case, you indicate how you could perform successfully in that position. In the latter, you indicate how your skills would be helpful in area A, B, or C.

The proposal of fit strategy assists the interviewer to move the discussion forward, and is helpful to you because it is based on your work and should afford you many opportunities to cite your successes. Let's consider the example of a clearly defined sales position, in which the candidate is seeing another in a line of interviewers:

> **Interviewer:** Have you discussed any of the specifics of our sales needs in your prior interviews?
>
> *Candidate:* I believe I have. There is a need for a sales person who is willing to demonstrate initiative in making sales calls, and overcoming the objections of a reluctant potential client.
>
> **Interviewer:** Yes, that's right. Do you think you can do that?
>
> *Candidate:* Yes, I do. I have demonstrated my ability to take risks when I was tornado tracking, and my success in Division I basketball has given me the self-assurance to deal with the objections of a reluctant potential client.
>
> **Interviewer:** If we hired you, what would you do first?
>
> *Candidate:* I would study every product in detail, and receive all the training help I could from successful sales people.
>
> **Interviewer:** Good.

This type of summary enables you to review prior meetings, so that the conversation can move forward instead of slipping backward.

A candidate who is crisp and to the point, uses time wisely, and helps the interviewer to move the discussion forward is likely to be successful. An additional benefit is that proactive candidates who are focused on how their skills and abilities can bring value to the company are much less likely to volunteer weaknesses. Candidates who are passive and reacting to questions are much more likely to be caught off-guard or seem ill prepared and more likely to volunteer weaknesses (often ones that are not even requested).

Tactics

- Be prepared to give examples of your relationship skills, your ability to work on a team, or to lead the team, if the situation calls for it.
- Make clear, crisp comments or answers to questions.
- Focus on the needs of the organization.
- Demonstrate how you can help solve the organization's problems.
- Be prepared to answer the questions, "What are your strongest competencies involving people?" and "What makes you unique?"

- Defend your accomplishments with people by using specific, bottom-line-oriented accomplishments.
- Synthesize information.
- Be a problem solver.
- Sell your skills and abilities to be successful.
- Use time wisely and efficiently.
- Project self-confidence (don't volunteer negatives.)
- Be positive.

Phase 4: Sell Candidate on the Company (and Resolve the Interviewer's Concerns)

Interviewer's Agenda:
- Sell candidate on the company.

Your Agenda:
- Test candidacy and overcome concerns.
- Ask good questions.

By this stage in the process, the interviewer has a strong sense of whether you are a viable candidate. One last question often asked is, "Tell me about one of your weaknesses." It is critical for you to spend time preparing the best possible answer. Ideally, you want to apply the following guidelines:

1. The response must be truthful.
2. Speak about something that is not fatal to your candidacy.
3. Explain how you have overcome, or how you are working to overcome the weakness.

An example might be, "I am driven and expect a great deal of myself." You have to be prepared for the interviewer to come back and ask if you are too hard on your yourself. You might say, "I have learned I cannot accomplish everything at once, and I prioritize better as I've gotten older."

Another example occurred when we interviewed a young manager in a chemical plant. When asked a weakness, he said, "I was not comfortable speaking before a group, so I took a public speaking course. Then I was able to practice my public speaking skills while communicating with the staff." This is a great answer; it is not only showing how he overcame a weakness, but it demonstrates a new skill that he has gained.

Assuming you are a good fit, interviewers normally transition to talking about their organizations. The "sell" is enthusiastic and warm. Interviewers answer your questions fully and attempt to put the company in the best possible light, while emphasizing the strengths of the organization. If you find yourself in this situation, enjoy it and use the time to learn more about the organization. This may also be a time when you can volunteer additional skills, abilities, or accomplishments to further your candidacy. Since the bonding process is continuing, you should do nothing to cut this process off.

In the alternative, if interviewers are not as sure whether you will continue in the process, you can probably tell. The answers to your questions are usually polite and short, without much additional information. If you really want this position, you have to make a serious attempt to overcome the interviewer's objections.

More likely, however, is the scenario where the interviewer perceives you have the skills and abilities to do the job, but isn't sure that you are a perfect fit. Indeed, few candidates are ever a perfect fit. This allows you the opportunity to test your candidacy and, if there are any concerns, to overcome them.

When someone thinks about raising and overcoming objections, it is often viewed as having to deal with real or perceived rejection. This isn't easy in any phase of life. It is tough when someone refuses to go out with you, when you lose an election, when the students don't seem to want to learn, or when a volunteer organization you believe in can't attract donations. The rejection of the product or the service organization, however, is nowhere near as difficult to deal with as the personal rejection felt in the date or the election. This is you, your very fiber, and it really hurts. The rejection in an interview, even if you have asked for problems to be brought to the surface, can feel like a personal rejection because you are talking about yourself, your skills, your abilities, your accomplishments, and your weaknesses.

Why then, would anyone go out to generate rejection? The answer is simple. Raising objections in an interview is not seeking rejection. Remember that you were screened before you ever got to the interview. You were deemed to be one of the best qualified of the applicants, or you would not have received an interview. Rejection is not associated with "best qualified."

Raising objections is a means of getting concerns out on the table while you're together. Then you have an opportunity to resolve them rather than leaving without knowing what concerns the interviewer might have. Earlier, we discussed asking for the ideal candidate characteristics as a means of setting the groundwork for this topic. Now it is possible to ask, "Mr. Jones, earlier I asked about the ideal personal and professional characteristics you have targeted. I feel I am a strong match. Can you tell me your reaction to my fit?"

Concerns fall into two basic categories: those you can fix and those you can't fix. A "can't fix" concern could be that the candidate must be a lawyer (which you're not) or have an MBA (which you don't.) A "can fix" concern is a comment like, "I'm not sure you have enough sales experience in your background." If most concerns fell into the "can't fix" category, we probably wouldn't raise the issue.

But that isn't the case. If you lacked a major skill set, you would never have been called in for an interview. Consequently, almost all concerns are in the "can fix" category, and the issue is one of clarification or explaining a skill set that hasn't been discussed in the interview. In response to the concern about sales experience, you might say, "Mr. Jones, we haven't had a chance to discuss my three years' sales and client service experience volunteering for my local hospital." Whether you need to clarify information or discuss a new skill set, it is a great opportunity for you. You're helping the interviewer learn more about your skills and abilities while clarifying misconceptions.

In addition, you have a unique opportunity to continue to build the relationship. Here is an opening to take a challenge, turn it to a positive that furthers your candidacy, and continue to build your relationship with the interviewer. That is a perfect opportunity to see how, if you were working for the company, you could deal with a client who was having an issue. The interviewer can actually observe how your thought process would work and how well you would handle yourself. Make sure you maintain eye contact with the interviewer during this part of the interview.

Having dealt with the weakness question and given you a chance to overcome objections, the interviewer will often ask if you have any questions about the company. You absolutely need to have questions, and you will be evaluated on your preparation in this area. The next chapter will present a number of appropriate questions. You will probably only be able to ask a few questions, so select the ones you think will be most appropriate.

Interview Tip! Overcoming Objections

Resolving a concern gives you a terrific opportunity to clarify something you said, to put forth additional skills, and to extend the interview.

Tactics

- Ask the interviewer what concerns he has with your candidacy.
- Have an answer for, "What is a weakness?"
- Don't take objections personally.
- Approach objections or concerns as a major opportunity.
- Maintain eye contact.
- Continue the conversation focusing on the positive.
- Deal with perceived weaknesses from a positive point of view (i.e., how have you overcome the weakness or how are you working on it.)
- Continue to gather data to evaluate the organization.
- Have outstanding questions to ask the interviewer.
- Be positive.

Phase 5: Close the Interview with Enthusiasm

Interviewer's Agenda:
- Close.

Your Agenda:
- Build rapport.
- Close.

Once the interviewer has accomplished his agenda, he may tell you about the next steps, and then close the meeting. Usually, the more he likes you, the more information you receive about upcoming events, such as additional interviews.

Openness and confidence should characterize your strategy for the close. This is a great opportunity to continue the bonding process with the interviewer. In addition, you have an opportunity to tell the interviewer anything else you feel is important to your candidacy. Just knowing you have this opportunity removes pressure during the interview. You want to thank the interviewer for taking the time to meet you, tell him about your excitement with the things he is doing (if you can say so truthfully,) and understand the timeframes and the process from this interview until the successful candidate is offered the job. Finally, if you are convinced you would like to work for the company, tell him, especially if he is your potential boss.

Interview Tip! Ask For The Job

Interviewing is no place for the timid. If you find a job you really want, and if you are qualified and well-prepared enough to get an interview, tell the interviewer you want to work for him.

Tactics

- Tell the interviewer how excited you are about the possibility of working with him.
- Remember that, if the interviewer "loves you," (in a business sense) anything is possible.
- Ask for the job.
- Understand the next steps in the interviewing process and the expected timelines.
- Obtain information that will help you in the upcoming interviews.
- Be positive.

Interview Tip! Positive Attitude

Interviewers look for positive, "can-do" candidates who are self-starters and eager to accept a challenge.

Summary

Within the interview framework, it is possible to implement strategies that increase the likelihood for success. Strategies must be used professionally, and within the comfort zone of the interviewer. You are not trying to take the meeting over; rather, you are looking for a chance to accomplish your agenda as well as help the interviewer accomplish his.

Key points of discussion are:
- Demonstrate Preparation, Presence, Presentation and Passion.
- Building rapport (by being approachable and interested and having fun) increases the chances of success.

- Consistently positive behavior in your presentation and content leaves a positive impression with the interviewer.
- A business discussion (50 percent talk each) is your best opportunity to accomplish your agenda.
- Test your candidacy and overcome objections.
- Have great questions for the interviewer.
- After selling your skills and abilities to assist the company achieve its objectives, ask for the job.
- Be positive.

Step 14: Your Questions for the Interviewer

Candidate questions are one of the best opportunities you will have to learn about the company, the position, and the people. It is an opportunity for you to assess:

- Intellectual honesty.
- Maturity, values, integrity.
- The quality of the management team.
- The challenge of the potential assignment.
- Consistency from interviewer to interviewer.
- Flaws in the "company's story."

The amount of time you have to ask your questions will depend upon a number of factors. In the screening interview, you may get little or no time to ask questions, but as you progress in the interview process, your leverage will increase.

A few potential interview questions you may want to ask are:

Company

- How do you measure success?
- What are your company's greatest strengths and needs?
- What are your company's "wow" factors?
- How are you perceived in the marketplace?
- What are the major issues facing your company in the next several years?
- Does your culture allow for disagreement? Could you give me an example?
- How would you describe the company's culture?
- How does your company show that what is said and what is practiced about mission, vision and values are in alignment?
- If I had an offer to work for an outstanding competitor of yours, such as a consulting firm or a top-tier investment bank, why should I choose your company?
- Why do people leave the organization?
- What is the average tenure at the firm?
- When you lose a candidate, where do they go? Why?

Position

- Can you describe the position I would fill? (If unknown or job description was not provided)

- What would you expect me to accomplish in the first year?
- What would be the major challenges for me in the first 12 months?
- Can you describe a situation that I might face and be expected to address?
- How do successful people gain the resources they need to perform successfully?
- What skills would I learn in the first 12-18 months?
- How would I be evaluated?
- Is there a chance to make a contribution to the overall effectiveness of the company and to have some visibility within a year or two? How?
- Does the company support a rotational process?
- Could you describe a realistic career path?
- Can you give me an example of the type of developmental assignment I might be offered after my initial assignment?
- Can you give me a feel for the compensation system and tell me why it is structured the way that it is?

Performance Review

- Would you describe the performance review process?
- How are performance expectations determined, and is mutual agreement important?
- To what degree will my bonus be tied to the performance review? How?
- Would you tell me about the talent review process that the company undertakes?
- Would the talent review include my level?
- What is the relationship between the talent review process and the performance evaluation?
- Will my compensation be tied to the talent review process?

People

- How does the company show people they are respected and valued?
- Please describe your orientation program.
- Can you give me an example that illustrates how your people exhibit the highest business ethics?
- How would you define the personal and professional characteristics of a successful person at your company?
- How do people have fun at work?
- Can you tell me about your formal and informal mentoring programs?

- Is effective coaching a mandatory requirement for supervisors?
- Will my boss encourage me to network?
- Will there by specific networking activities for new hires? Cross-department and cross-divisional as well?
- Do you believe in continuous learning? If so, what kind of training could I expect?
- What types of training programs have been most successful?
- How would you help me to develop my leadership skills?
- Is the supervisor's promotion dependent, to some degree, on his/her hiring and promotion record? Can you give me an example?
- Is it important to you to see your people promoted to "stretch" assignments, even if it means moving to a new area? Can you give me an example of where that happened?

Step 15: Evaluate Your Performance

Competitive interviewing requires the measurement of your progress against your objectives, and should even occur during the interview.

Psychologists tell us we can remember only a limited number of things in short-term memory. Therefore, we have settled on the three basic objectives mentioned previously:
- **Presence:** Build rapport with the interviewer.
- **Presentation:** Accomplish the interviewer's agenda—present your professional and personal skills clearly and concisely.
- **Passion:** Accomplish your agenda—demonstrate your passion for work and life, convince the interviewer that you have the skills to perform successfully, and are the outstanding candidate.

These objectives can be managed during the interview. Any more than this and your energy is focused on remembering objectives rather than on the interview.

Immediately prior to the interview (for preparation and review) the "Two Minute Drill" is helpful. After the interview, the longer evaluation check-list of your performance, presented in this chapter, is of great value. It is helpful for at least two reasons.

First, since people tend to be extremely self-critical, the objectivity of an evaluation tool helps to keep an interview in proper perspective. Often, you realize you did a better job than you thought. Second, complete self-assessment has a positive long-term effect. It immediately reinforces positive behaviors and points to necessary changes in the next interview.

Quick Evaluation: During the Interview

We have been discussing these concepts since the beginning of the book. Since they are practical and simple, they become an integral part of your interview routine. A simple mental determination—"accomplished" or "not accomplished"—every so often during the interview gives you indication of where you are. A "not accomplished" indicates an opportunity. The mental score board looks like this:

Objective 1: Presence—Recognize the importance of building rapport. Did we discover and discuss one or two common interests, acquaintances, or experiences?

Objective 2: Presentation—Accomplish the interviewer's agenda.
Did the interviewer learn my three or four strongest competencies, did I have 5 accomplishments for each competency and did I support them with bottom-line results?

Objective 3: Passion—Accomplish your agenda.
Did I identify three or four of the organization's most critical needs, and convince the interviewer that I have the energy, motivation, and drive, that I would love to work at this company, and sell my skills and abilities to perform successfully?

As you mentally check the scoreboard at various points in the meeting, you can gauge what you have to accomplish. Then, using the strategies and tactics discussed in the last chapter, you can make it happen. It's simple and it works.

Full Evaluation: After the Interview

After the interview, look at the three basic objectives and the criteria that comprise them. Evaluate the criteria one at a time using a ranking of 1 to 5 (5 being high).

Objective 1: Presence—Recognize the importance of building rapport.
Did we discover and discuss one or two common interests, acquaintances, or experiences?

Personal Interaction
- The interviewer made me feel comfortable.   1 2 3 4 5
- I made the interviewer feel comfortable.   1 2 3 4 5
- The interviewer smiled or laughed.   1 2 3 4 5
- I smiled or laughed.   1 2 3 4 5
- The interviewer was comfortable with herself.   1 2 3 4 5
- The interviewer made eye contact.   1 2 3 4 5
- I made eye contact.   1 2 3 4 5
- The interviewer was open and sincere.   1 2 3 4 5
- I was open and sincere with the interviewer.   1 2 3 4 5
- I felt free to ask questions.   1 2 3 4 5
- I was able to express my ideas openly.   1 2 3 4 5
- We identified common interests.   1 2 3 4 5
- We identified common friends or acquaintances.   1 2 3 4 5
- We discussed common experiences.   1 2 3 4 5

Professional Issues
- The interviewer seems to enjoy working for the company.   1 2 3 4 5
- The interviewer seems to enjoy her job.   1 2 3 4 5
- I would want to work for this person.   1 2 3 4 5
- The interviewer was willing to give me information   1 2 3 4 5
  about the company (bad as well as good.)

Building rapport is a two-way street. If the interviewer is comfortable with the process, she may take the lead. If not, it may fall to you to keep the conversation going. "Why me?" you might ask; "That's the interviewer's role." That may be true in a theoretical sense, but it is irrelevant in reality.

Career Profile
Assisting the Interviewer

It was obvious to Jorge, a candidate for a finance position with the U.S. government Treasury Department, that Marge, his potential boss, was uneasy in her role as interviewer. Marge greeted Jorge stiffly after her secretary brought him to her office. Marge sat behind the protection of her large desk, peering over the top of a lot of files. Halting small talk lasted less than three minutes (it seemed like an hour) before Marge mercifully turned the discussion to business.

Jorge was wise enough to understand that rapport building is an ongoing theme throughout the interview. As the interview progressed, Jorge learned that Marge had been in her job less than a year and this was her first hire. Jorge felt that Marge seemed shy, in addition to being uncomfortable with her responsibility to recruit and hire someone. Jorge was not very comfortable himself (who would be?), but he did his best to appear relaxed.

When Marge asked a question, Jorge tried to give a little extra detail in the hope of hitting a responsive chord (still less than 60 seconds) and he tried to smile when appropriate. (Note: Marge later admitted that informal conversation was extremely difficult for her; so you can imagine how Jorge must have felt.) Finally, Marge asked Jorge a question about why he hadn't taken a position in the West where he went to school. Jorge said, "My girlfriend's father was ill and, since he was alone, Sue felt she needed to be close to him. That required a move from Colorado back to Virginia and we wanted to be together, so I resigned.

Before we came back, however, we took three weeks to take one last white water rafting trip."

That last sentence Jorge added could have been nothing more than a little color, but it was the one that lit up the scoreboard. Marge's expression changed, and she came alive.

"You went white water rafting in Colorado?" she asked.

"Yes," said Jorge, "on the Arkansas and the Colorado rivers. It was our favorite recreational activity."

Marge loved the outdoors. She and her husband had gone white water canoeing on most of the major rivers in the East and were planning their first trip to the West. Marge completely forgot her heavily structured interview (every question had been listed on a sheet of paper,) and she wanted to know about rafting on the Arkansas. Jorge was happy to tell her about travel arrangements, places to stay, and the best guides. The conversation wasn't difficult anymore.

After thoroughly discussing her summer plans, Marge suggested they return to the business discussion (Jorge would never have cut off the rafting discussion.) Now, however, the interview became a relaxed business conversation rather than the uncomfortable question/answer format. Jorge was able to ask a number of questions, and could then focus his answers on Marge's business concerns.

Jorge had a series of interviews with Marge's boss and others in Marge's department, but he felt he had won the job in that interview when the discussion turned to white water rafting. Marge later verified that his feeling was correct. She said she was scared to death hiring her first person and Jorge not only had the necessary skills, but also helped her overcome her nervousness. His patience and concern for the interviewer's comfort won the day.

Objective 2: Presentation--Accomplish the interviewer's agenda.
Did I present my three or four strongest competencies and did I support them with 5 accomplishments to illustrate each competency with bottom-line accomplishments?

Personal/Professional Skills
- I was direct and to the point.   1 2 3 4 5
- The interviewer appeared to be satisfied that I specifically   1 2 3 4 5
  and concisely answered questions.
- I have the following evidence to support that assessment.   1 2 3 4 5
- I followed the basic principle that no answer should be   1 2 3 4 5
  longer than 60 seconds.
- The interviewer did not have to clarify or repeat questions.   1 2 3 4 5
- I cited skills and abilities that were relevant to the job needs. 1 2 3 4 5
- The interviewer gained a clear picture of my strongest   1 2 3 4 5
  professional and personal skills.
- My examples were bottom-line-oriented.   1 2 3 4 5
- I demonstrated my ability to learn new skills quickly.   1 2 3 4 5
- I gave strong examples of my flexibility and adaptability.   1 2 3 4 5
- My leadership and management potential were discussed.   1 2 3 4 5

A real concern in the interview occurs right after the transition from rapport building to the business portion of the meeting. You need to help the interviewer attain a comfort level, even if it means holding back on your agenda for more time than feels comfortable. Richard put himself in a difficult position on just this issue.

Career Profile
Reading the Cues

Richard was interviewing with Sylvia for a marketing position. Rapport building had gone smoothly. The discussion was conversational in tone and very relaxed. It was clear to Richard that Sylvia liked him.

As Sylvia made the transition to the business portion of the meeting, Richard was feeling very confident. Things had been so relaxed to this point he was sure he'd be able to get Sylvia to talk about the business needs of her department. He made the fatal mistake of assuming that a relaxed, conversational style in the rapport-building phase would automatically carry over to the initial phases of the business meeting.

Instead of assisting Sylvia to reach a comfort level, he tried to get at her business needs too early. When he started to ask her questions before she was ready, she reverted to a typical question/answer style, which signaled to him that she was uncomfortable with his behavior. Fortunately, he immediately realized what he had done. He had lost sight of helping Sylvia with her agenda in an effort to accomplish his own.

At this point he had lost most of the rapport he had developed earlier. Rather than push further, he just followed Sylvia's lead. When she asked questions about his accomplishments, Richard kept his answers short because he realized he had not yet let her completely cover her needs. As time went on, she began to become more comfortable again. By the last one-third of the meeting they were involved in an intense business discussion. Sylvia told Richard the major needs of her department and, sure enough, they were different from what Richard's intelligence had provided. He was pleased he had kept his answers short. Now that he knew the real needs, he was able to target his accomplishments to Sylvia's needs.

When he left the interview, Richard was upset with himself. He should have known better than to press too soon. Yet, on the positive side, he had seemed to save the day. He mentally gave himself a B for the interview (it felt a lot better three interviews later when he was hired.)

"How I was able to help the interviewer?" is in many ways the most difficult objective to self-evaluate. How do you know whether you are focusing on the interviewer's interests? To get at this, you have to focus on the things you can control, such as your ability to listen, to respond to a question, to give clear answers, and to keep the answers short.

Objective 3: Passion--Accomplish your agenda.
Did I identify three or four of the organization's most critical needs, and convince the interviewer that I have the energy, motivation and drive, that I would love to work for this company, and sell my skills and abilities to perform successfully?

Identify needs
- Each of us spoke about 50 percent of the time in each   1 2 3 4 5
  phase of the interview.
- I was comfortable asking questions.   1 2 3 4 5
- The questions generated needs.   1 2 3 4 5
- The questions were insightful and were a natural   1 2 3 4 5
  outgrowth of the conversation.
- The interview remained in an easy, give-and-take   1 2 3 4 5
  conversational style.

Confirm needs
- I confirmed the organization's needs.   1 2 3 4 5
- I was able to generate additional needs during this   1 2 3 4 5
  portion of the meeting.
- My initial hunches concerning needs were correct.   1 2 3 4 5

Sell abilities
- I was clear and concise in my presentation.   1 2 3 4 5
- I maintained the interviewer's interest as I presented   1 2 3 4 5
  my skills and abilities.
- The interviewer was interested and involved.   1 2 3 4 5
- I cited statistics that demonstrated how my contributions   1 2 3 4 5
  impacted the bottom line.
- I told the interviewer I wanted to work for her.   1 2 3 4 5
- I asked for the job.   1 2 3 4 5

Career Profile
Accomplish Your Agenda

Carlos was extremely pleased with the way the interview was going. As he did a quick mental check, he had clearly built outstanding rapport with Dan, his potential boss at the public relations firm. They had spent more time than Carlos expected, and the conversation felt relaxed and productive.

Dan made the transition easily to the business portion of the meeting, and he began to question Carlos on his professional skills. Carlos felt he answered the questions well about his academic training and specialized skills. When Dan asked for an example of where Carlos had used public relations skills at school, he felt he had an excellent answer. He told Dan how the international students' club had fallen on hard times before Carlos arrived at school, and a group of students wanted to revive it. Once on campus, Carlos became interested and involved in the revival effort and he told Dan five of the techniques he had employed in an effort to build publicity for the club. Dan did not have to ask for bottom line results because Carlos told him about the 300 percent increase in membership in the first two years of the club's revival.

As the interview progressed, Carlos saw pockets of opportunity to ask Dan questions. One question was, "Can you give me an idea of your ideal candidate?" and another was, "What are the major challenges that the successful candidate will face in the first year on the job?" Dan smiled and appreciated Carlos asking the question. He was open and forthcoming about the challenges that lay ahead. Carlos was proud of himself for successfully and smoothly drawing out the needs. As he was about to follow that question with a presentation of his skills and abilities to accomplish them, Dan was interrupted by his administrative assistant. She apologized as she asked if Dan could step out for a moment. Within 3 minutes, Dan returned and was very apologetic about the interruption. "She only does that in an emergency," he said. For Carlos, the interruption made him lose his focus, and he totally forgot to complete the sell of how his skills and abilities were perfect for Dan's position.

On his way home, Carlos thought about the opportunity he had missed, and he was disappointed with himself. Before he reached home, however, he recalled the value of the thank you note and thought he might be able to save his candidacy. By that evening, Carlos had completed a thank you note that he e-mailed to Dan. His note took each one of the challenges that Dan identified and presented his skills and abilities to attack the problem. When Carlos completed the task, he was surprised to see there were two of his skill sets that had not been discussed during the course of the interview.

Carlos felt a huge sense of relief when he received a call from Dan's administrative assistant a few days later with a request for him to come in for another interview. Within a few weeks, he received an offer and was able to put his skills into practice.

Summary

Evaluation is most productive if it is accomplished during the interview. A simple mental assessment at various points during the interview helps you to assess how you are progressing. If you need a course correction, you can utilize the appropriate strategies and tactics to accomplish your goals.

The objectives are:
- **Objective 1: Presence--Build rapport with the interviewer**.
  Did we discover and discuss one or two common interests, acquaintances, or experiences?

- **Objective 2: Presentation—Accomplish the interviewer's agenda.**
  Did the interviewer learn my three or four strongest competencies; did I have 5 accomplishments for each competency, and did I support them with bottom-line accomplishments?
- **Objective 3: Passion—Accomplish your agenda.**
  Did I identify three or four of the organization's most critical needs, and convince the interviewer that I have the energy, motivation and drive, that I would love to work for the company, and did I sell my skills and abilities to perform?

Prior to the interview, a review of the "The Two Minute Drill" is beneficial. After the interview, the in-depth analysis presented in this chapter can serve to reinforce your positive behaviors and assist with course corrections for the next interview.

Step 16: The After-the-Interview Checklist

After each interview, you need to send a thank you letter or email to each person you met. The guideline is that the effect of the thank you letter is lost if the interviewer doesn't receive it within five business days.

You will need to make a decision as to the type of letter you want to send. There is no clear research regarding e-mail, typed, or hand written, so you will want to make a decision based on your intuition of what the receiver would value.

Thank you letter—Within 5 Business Days

A thank you letter to each interviewer should be considered an extension of the interview—and an absolute necessity. Few job applicants do this, and it really makes a difference. The thank you letter is usually a few paragraphs in length with each paragraph covering a different topic. The letter should not be more than one side of an e-mail or page.

The initial sentence should refer to something specific from your conversation so that it becomes a personal, rather than a business letter. You might say: "I enjoyed meeting you and learning about your objectives..." or "Thank you for meeting with me and sharing your thoughts on the direction of the company." Then indicate your interest and excitement in the position and the company.

The second paragraph is an opportunity to reinforce those of your beliefs that agree with the company's direction or methodology. It's a way to continue bonding with the interviewer and to indicate that you are in sync with the company. This can include ways your skills could be helpful going forward.

The third paragraph is optional. This is a chance to mention your skills and abilities that were not discussed during the interview, but that you feel will further your candidacy. Sometimes, a critical skill or ability was not discussed due to time constraints or due to the direction of the conversation. This is an opportunity to rectify the oversight.

The final paragraph is a review of the next steps and a closing. You might end, for example, with "I look forward to hearing from you in a week to schedule the next interviews."

Interview Tip! Thank You Letter

You have five business days to have a thank you letter on each interviewer's desk or you lose the value of the letter.

Occasionally, you might be given an assignment to complete as part of the evaluative process. It could be for a writing sample, your apparel designs, or sample of your marketing products. You might also be asked for a proposal of how you would tackle a problem or even start a business. Assignments should be of the highest quality, presented in a professional style, and completed on time.

Your short-term follow-up should relate to interview content and timing. It may be your responsibility to call back for another interview, for example. If you reach the interviewer, express your excitement about coming back and your interest in the position. Also, ask if any additional information is needed to further your candidacy.

Ongoing follow-up is in your hands. Assuming that the position will be filled in the near term, a call back in 7-10 days is not considered too much. A call is fine, or you might send the interviewer an article you found that relates to his industry or company. The objective is to remain front of mind on the interviewer's radar screen.

Campaign administration is critical at this juncture. Your organization and daily planning track when you need to make follow-up calls, complete assignments or appear for interviews. Perseverance and determination will pay off and positive attitude when you meet someone will win the job.

PART VI

Selecting the Company

The premise of the buy side is: "As a prospective employee, I have as much responsibility to judge and evaluate prospective employers as they do to judge and evaluate me. If the employer and I both do our jobs well, we both enhance the likelihood of achieving a great match." Top candidates want:

- A dynamic, highly successful and demanding organization.
- Challenging and exciting work.
- Outstanding boss, mentor and coach.
- A team that respects me as an individual and wants me as a partner.
- Competitive compensation and benefits.
- A reasonable work/life balance.

Step 17: What Outstanding Candidates Seek in a Job

The buy side of the equation is often neglected, in whole or in part, by prospective job seekers. To repeat, the premise of the buy side study goes like this: "As a prospective employee, I have as much responsibility to judge and evaluate prospective employers as they do to judge and evaluate me. If the employer and I both do our jobs well, we both enhance the likelihood of achieving a great match." The reason for needing to make a good decision is clear. There are only a finite number of career decisions and/or moves to make during the course of a business career.

Most people agree that they are happier, more content, and easier to live with when:
- They are in a challenging job.
- They are learning new skills.
- Their company is doing well.
- They work with bright, stimulating, and fun people.
- They can visualize a career path.

Any time someone is in transition from college to the job market, coming back into the job market, or making a job change, their normal life equilibrium is temporarily thrown out of balance. The imbalance can last a short time if a good career choice is made, or a long time if a poor choice is made. Not only can a poor choice make you unhappy, but it can also hold back your career progress. That's why the buy side of the decision is so important.

In this chapter we will discuss what top job candidates want in a job. Keep in mind that your evaluation will be based on research that you have done, networking with people who have knowledge of the company and, most important, your evaluation of the interviewers who represent the company, its mission, and values. In the next chapter, we'll discuss the characteristics of outstanding interviewers. Top candidates want:
- A dynamic, highly successful, and demanding organization with a strong corporate culture.
- Challenging and exciting work with continuous learning.
- An outstanding boss, mentor, and coach.
- A team that respects me as an individual and wants me as a partner.
- Competitive compensation and benefits.
- A reasonable work/life balance.

A Dynamic, Highly Successful, and Demanding Organization with a Strong Corporate Culture

A top candidate wants to work for a company that provides something more than a place to go to work. He wants a challenging job in a great company, a company on the rise, or a company that is committed to turning itself in a new direction. Many job seekers also seek to improve the human condition through the products or services they provide.

In Merck & Co.'s corporate headquarters, for example, there is a life-size statue of a small boy leading a blind man. The statue is so realistic and compelling that everyone is immediately drawn to it. The inscription states that Merck developed an inoculation to prevent river blindness disease. When it became apparent that many of the developing nations in Africa had neither the finances nor the communication mechanisms to eradicate river blindness, Merck donated the vaccine and has contributed manpower and dollars to lessen the impact of the disease.

Everyone knows that Merck & Co. is one of the top pharmaceutical companies in the world. Everyone may not know about their philanthropic outreaches. When a top candidate, who is interested in a job that also offers the opportunity to give something back to humankind, walks into Merck's lobby, the statue with its inscription is sure to make a powerful statement.

Challenging and Exciting Work with Continuous Learning

Imagine the rush you would feel if you were one of the contributors to a recent NASA space mission. Your work would be of great interest to others. You would be on the cutting edge of technology with a challenging job that places you in the forefront of learning new and marketable skills. In addition, your work would be designed to bring greater good to humankind.

Those who work at NASA agree with the components we just mentioned. They also add that working on a highly sophisticated project with a committed, smart, high-energy team is a great deal of fun as well. In addition, there is energy generated from having a big goal driven by a "we can do anything" mentality. Work is as much a happening as it is a job.

You don't have to work at NASA to have such an experience. You can find many places where you will find great excitement, challenging work, continuous learning, and a chance to build a company. This can happen in many different ways. It can be a small, growing advertising agency that is built vertically so that the team works on assignments together, giving everyone a chance to grow. It can be an Internet startup with all of the energy inherent in working on a new idea with a group of smart people. It can also happen within a large division of an established company or a small project team where a committed group of people take on a challenging assignment, and have the resources to make it happen.

Career profile
Learning and Growing

Naya Collins took a job as an E-commerce manager in the arts and entertainment industry 14 months ago. When asked what her goal is for five years from now, she answers that it is of utmost importance that she continues to enjoy what she's doing and have personal satisfaction. "If I'm not learning and growing every single day, then I'm out of here," she says. It is interesting that the goal doesn't include "making partner in five years," or "hoping to make my first million by my thirty-second birthday."

Outstanding Boss, Mentor, and Coach

The leadership literature over the last quarter century has been clear—the boss is one of the most important criteria in someone's success or failure in the job. So, finding the right boss is critical. Today's most successful bosses have moved to a more participative leadership style, and away from a vertical, authoritative style. This is not only in keeping with leadership research, but is a style, that is more effective with today's young professionals.

This participative style is very consistent with hard work and productivity. Young job seekers enjoy challenging work, and they are willing to take on both additional freedom and accountability. In fact, they want to work in a performance-based environment where one is paid for productivity. However, a productive state can be reached much more quickly if the boss is positive and supportive.

With an initial sense of security, the new hire can approach the things she needs to learn about the organization. Knowing the short- and long-term goals of the organization and why they are the goals is important. She needs to know what is expected in her job, and she needs both freedom and guidance to move forward. She also needs feedback concerning her personal successes and failures, including suggestions for improvement.

As she gains experience in the environment, she needs an opportunity for greater independence. She wants to accept authority and responsibility for her work as well as accountability for what she does. Independence allows stretching and the development of new capabilities and skills. Achieving success through these efforts produces a larger degree of satisfaction from work.

Bosses who can support these transitions are special individuals. They need to be mature, fair, and self-confident. They must understand the need for assistance early in one's tenure with a company, and the need to allow independence as soon as possible. They must believe in training and development as a means to growth. It is a great benefit to have a boss who is proud of the number of his subordinates who have been promoted within the organization. Finally, if a new hire can find a boss who will be her mentor, then she has hit the jackpot.

A Team That Respects Me as an Individual and Wants Me as a Partner

Respect is assessed in a very practical, comparative manner: How am I being treated by this company in comparison to how other companies treat me?

Your initial reaction will be to see how you are treated. The members of the recruiting team should be hand selected for their ability to make you feel comfortable, build rapport, and have an intuitive sense about doing the right thing when it comes to human relationships. Their maturity, sense of self worth, and love of their work should come through in the interview.

It is often difficult to learn the real information about the organization from watching members of the interview team alone. So you will want to keep your antenna up as you move about the company to see how people treat each other. It can be as simple as whether people are friendly toward each other as they walk down the hall, or how interviewers talk about current staff and those who left the company.

In terms of your potential team, you want to assess whether the team will accept you, help you to learn your job, and give you time to progress along the learning curve. You will gain a sense of these things by the discussion you have, and by the questions you ask. You also want to hear evidence of the team having some fun together, in addition to working hard and being productive.

Career Profile
Team Respect

Naveen's decision came down to two firms, one a large prestigious firm and the other a small, highly regarded consulting firm. He ultimately accepted with the consulting firm because he learned that even the newest employees are involved in aspects of the firm's decision making. Everyone gets close to the clients and there is some flexibility in work schedules. The partners regularly entertain employees in their own homes, rather than keeping staff at arm's length.

Competitive Compensation and Benefits

Fair compensation is important to everyone. With little effort, you can find out what a company pays new or young employees at your level. There are salary surveys online or you can network with friends who will give you competitive salary data. Due to the ease of gaining this information, large companies often pay entry-level associates at the same rate. In some organizations, this is not an issue. School systems, for example, have a salary guide that identifies a specific salary at a given experience level.

Many professionals, however, want to be rewarded for their individual contributions in addition to the contribution of their department. You need to decide your position on this matter so you do not end up in a company whose compensation system and benefits will frustrate you. Some firms pay sales professionals on a salary and bonus structure, while others pay salary and commission, and some pay straight commission. There are trade-offs to each of the systems, and it is important to know where you will be happy.

A Reasonable Work/Life Balance

Reasonable work/life balance is very much an individual decision. If you are driven to pursue a career path based on growth up the corporate ladder in a fast paced company that is recognized as an industry leader, then you must be prepared to have less work/life balance. As you grow and are promoted you will make more money, spend a lot of time at work (probably,) and work will be a greater part of your life.

Many young professionals, today, are willing to make tradeoffs that improve the work/life equation. "I don't need to work 12 and 14 hour days, or be on a fast track, or be the CEO some day," they say. I'm more interested in working for a company that provides a product or service that will help humankind where I can make a reasonable to good living, and still have time for family, as well as religious and community activities.

In either case, you need time to meet personal and family commitments. If a boss or firm will not provide for reasonable needs in this area, you need to decide whether it is the right firm for you. Other considerations include where (geographically) to live, pace of work, and degree of flexibility of when and where you work.

Summary

Outstanding candidates want specific criteria when they select a job. They are:

- A dynamic, highly successful, and demanding organization with a strong corporate culture.
- Challenging and exciting work with continuous learning.
- An outstanding boss, mentor, and coach.
- A team that respects me as an individual and wants me as a partner.
- Competitive compensation and benefits.
- A reasonable work/life balance.

Step 18: The Characteristics of Outstanding Interviewers

Kristina agreed to the interview in a small consulting firm solely to please Liz, her best friend. She had already conducted a thorough, effective job search, and had arrived at her decision about a job within three months. She attributed some of her short job campaign to luck, but she knew it was also due in to an excellent educational background, strong experience, and an extremely positive attitude. She had done everything except give her final acceptance to her new employer, and the company wanted her to start as soon as possible.

She was prepared to cancel the interview when Liz told her it would be personally embarrassing to her if Kristina did not go through with it, since she had gone to great lengths to arrange the meeting. Liz was clear that all she wanted was for Kristina to go through the motions.

Kristina met the chairman first, who was known to be a positive, high-energy person who could see the bright side of any situation. Winston was well-dressed and emitted self-confidence. The conversation initially focused on the history of Winston's small, high quality consulting company, and then moved to of-the-moment issues facing the consulting industry. Although she came with zero expectations, Kristina felt herself drawn into the conversation and even felt a little excited. The excitement was tempered, however, by the reality that she was committed to another company. Eventually, she felt compelled to tell Winston about her commitment. For a moment, Winston looked surprised, but he quickly continued on with the conversation.

When they finished a two-hour conversation, Winston asked Kristina to meet the head of the Chicago office, who was right down the hall. Kristina was pleased that she had been honest with Winston about her situation, but she was clearly excited by their conversation and since she had ample time that day, she said, "I'd be happy to meet him." Within a few minutes George appeared, and invited Kristina to his office.

She was impressed by George's intelligence and insight into the issues facing the company. Clearly, Winston's firm was at a cross-road; it would have to grow by hiring the right people or through acquisition, or it would be swallowed up by a larger firm. Winston and the professionals in the firm had decided they wanted to control their own fate. They were well on their way to becoming larger and more viable.

By the time Kristina returned to Winston's office an hour later, he had lined up three more people for her to meet. Kristina was too intrigued to say no at this point. She met Pamela next, and it was an instant replay of the meeting with George. They hit it off immediately, and had a great meeting, comparing notes and sharing ideas about the state of the industry. Pamela was smart, fit, professional, outgoing, positive, and energetic. She had some exciting clients, and the assignments she was working on sounded particularly challenging.

Kristina completed the last two interviews that afternoon, and they were more of the same. Instead of feeling tired, as had happened in past interviews with other companies, Kristina found herself completely energized. Winston saw her on the way out, and told her that his people were very enthusiastic about her. He asked if she could come back the next day to meet some more people. He never mentioned Kristina's job offer. As it turned out, Kristina had plans for the next day, but they agreed to continue the dialogue the day after.

Within that three-day period, Kristina had a dozen interviews. She was fortunate to meet at least one person from the New York, San Francisco, and Atlanta offices who happened to be traveling through Chicago. By the end of the interviews, she had a second job offer.

When Kristina went home at the end of the interviews, she was shocked at what had happened. A required appearance had turned into a dozen interviews and a job offer. The more she thought about what happened, the more she realized she was much more like these people than those in the company that made her the first offer. Her immediate reaction was dismay. She felt as though she had sold out the first company by continuing the interview process. She came to the conclusion that she owed it to the first company to go to work for them, but her heart was with Winston's group.

Then Liz called to ask what had happened. When Kristina told her, Liz laughed. "I've heard that reaction before," Liz said. "There is something magnetic about Winston and his colleagues."

When Kristina told Liz about her dilemma, Liz asked her a question. "Have you started work for them?" she asked.

Kristina responded, "No, I haven't even officially accepted. But I certainly gave every indication that I would." Liz suggested that Kristina go back to the first company, see the person who would be her direct boss, and explain that she had received another offer that better fit her career goals.

Kristina knew that it would be a difficult conversation, but she knew she couldn't pass on the opportunity to work with Winston's group. She was able to schedule the meeting the next day. The meeting went reasonably well and her potential boss was professional, although she was clearly disappointed.

That afternoon, Kristina called Winston and excitedly accepted his position. When they got together, Winston asked why she accepted his offer. Kristina told Winston that she had spent a lot of time thinking about that in the last 72 hours. She responded, "I was struck by the intelligence, skills, and experience of the staff. I believe I can learn from them, and perhaps share some things I have learned. There is an amazing sense of energy and everyone is so positive and 'can-do.' I think that outlook is a must in a consulting environment. Perhaps most important for me, however, is that I think you and your people are great. I absolutely want to work with you."

This case study illustrates an important point in your evaluation. Kristina was an intelligent, thoughtful candidate who used an analytical and systematic approach to her job search. The variable that adds a new dimension that is unpredictable and emotional is people.

Interpersonal dynamics becomes an important ingredient in the ultimate decision. You will be interviewed at great companies by highly professional interview teams who are outstanding at selling candidates on the merits of their companies. It is a difficult process to make the buy decision for a particular company, especially if you are just graduating from college and have no experience. Interpersonal dynamics emerge when you are more closely drawn to one interviewer or interview team than to another.

You may be saying now, "But I thought this book was about building a partnership with the interviewer. Now, if I've done that you're saying be careful." That is a good thought. That is exactly what this book is about. It is outstanding to build an excellent relationship with one or more interviewers, and an excellent criteria in your decision making process is the boss and your work team. All we are saying is you will need to have your most sensitive antennae and intuition when it comes to evaluating interviewers to determine whether they will be good business partners. And, don't forget to evaluate the other criteria that we discussed in the last chapter.

Before examining the characteristics of outstanding interviewers, we want to review what behavioral research teaches us regarding human drives and motivators. The research further drives home the importance of understanding that emotion is an important aspect of the "buy" decision. By keeping these things in mind, you will be better able to be objective in evaluating all aspects of a position, and not just how one interviewer makes you feel, versus another. For example, one interviewer may actually have a better company and job, but may not be as engaging an interviewer as another.

Behavioral Research

- We are ego-centered and seek praise. (If someone wants to praise something that I have done, I am usually going to react well to the comment and the person.)
- We think of ourselves as winners. (I am likely to rate myself higher in self-evaluation surveys than might truly be the case.)
- We are strongly driven from within and self-motivated. (I am capable of being a self-starter who seeks to be highly productive.)
- We act as if express beliefs are important, yet actions speak louder than words (I will not miss any of your actions and they will tell me, more than your words, whether you respect and value me.)
- We profoundly need meaning in our lives and will sacrifice a great deal to institutions that will provide it. (I want to work for a company that makes products I am proud of and for which I will go the extra distance.)

With the behavioral research in mind as a reminder of what motivates us, you are now in a position to recognize the characteristics of outstanding interviewers so you can make the best "buy" decision. The interviewers in the case studies that follow go beyond their normal job duties and demonstrate the characteristics of outstanding interviewers, the kind whose company you may want to join.

The Characteristics of Outstanding Interviewers

Highest character: integrity and maturity

Maria couldn't have been happier with her decision. She decided just before Christmas to join the human resources department of the conglomerate in her home state of Alabama. She was to join one of the divisions as an associate in employee relations in June, after graduation.

From the time Maria agreed to join the firm, her new boss put Maria on the mailing list for the company newsletters, the annual report, and other special publications. As Maria read the newsletter in the early spring, she began to get an uneasy feeling. It seemed that the division's profitability had declined, and a management study had been undertaken to evaluate the problem.

Maria wasn't sure what to do. As a new employee, she didn't think she should be calling her boss, but the future of the division was of critical importance to her. Shortly thereafter, the telephone rang. It was Ralph, the vice president of human resources, who was reaching out to communicate with her. After some initial pleasantries, Ralph confirmed that the division wasn't doing well. It seemed that new technology was changing the way the industry operated and the division was behind the technology curve.

He told Maria the company still very much wanted her but, in an effort to be honest, he told her there was a possibility the division could be sold or merged with another division, and moved to a new location. Maria asked Ralph what he thought she should do. They had an open discussion; Ralph asked her how important it was for her to move back to that part of Alabama. She indicated that it was very important because her fiancé lived there. Ralph advised her to conduct a job search for other opportunities in the city and to remain in close contact with him so he could inform her of developments within his company.

Within three months, Maria had two other offers, although they were not as appealing as Ralph's. She felt a little apprehensive about calling Ralph, but she did and told him about the other offers. He was very understanding. He then said that there were better business signs at his division. The technology they lacked had been developed much more quickly than expected, and there was an 85 percent probability that the division would not be sold or moved. He was careful to underscore, however, that it was 85 percent and not 100 percent.

He indicated he thought her job was safe, and that he still wanted her to join the company. Maria was excited as she thanked Ralph for communicating openly and honestly with her. She stuck with her decision to join Ralph's team and went to work shortly thereafter.

Self-awareness: Exercises self-control and has knowledge of company strengths and weaknesses

Joseph knew every strength of his large conglomerate as well as each perceived weakness that would be thrown back at him as he prepared for his presentation to MBA students at a highly acclaimed graduate school. He knew the students would be direct, and that challenging work, a chance to learn cutting-edge skills, and an opportunity to make an impact quickly would be important to them.

The presentation went extremely well, and after it was over, Joseph welcomed questions from the students. It didn't take long before the discussion focused on a comparison of working for a large company, a consulting firm, or an investment bank. A student asked, "Granted, your firm has a great reputation; but many of my classmates are focused on consulting, due to the variety of assignments across a range of industries, or investment banking, to learn cutting-edge finance. Aren't they compelling reasons?"

The boldness of the remark caused a momentary hush in the room as the students waited for Joseph's response. Almost instantly, a huge smile crossed Joseph's face and he said, "They certainly are. If you were to join our company you'd have a chance to do both. As you may know, we rotate executives through a series of positions in an effort to expose them to a broad range of opportunities so they can get close to the business. We are proud of the reputation we have earned as being at the cutting-edge of finance. As you grow with us, you would be in an excellent position to become a line manager and run your own business."

Joseph knew how well he had responded when there was spontaneous applause from the students.

Being centered: balanced with strong business ethics and values

Ted had hit a wall in his efforts to recruit Erik. He had done everything he could think of, and wasn't sure if he had made any significant headway. Ted knew that Erik was in real demand, and had three other offers.

One day, he decided to have lunch with an old friend. Once they caught up on personal issues, they began to discuss business issues. Eventually, Ted mentioned the problem he was having recruiting a highly desirable candidate. His friend asked about the college the student was attending. Ted responded, "The University of Texas."

His friend thought for a moment and said, "We don't get too many from that part of the country, but we did recruit one young man from Texas a few years ago. I think he was a football player." Ted told his friend that Erik was a basketball player.

That afternoon, Ted's friend called him and said he had spoken to the former football player from Texas. His friend asked Ted if he'd like to speak with him. "Sure," Ted responded. Ted learned that the former football player, Jay, had friends at Texas who were very close to the basketball coach. Ted asked if Jay would assist him and if his friends could make a connection with the coach. Within a short time, Ted had been introduced to the basketball coach via telephone, and they agreed to meet.

They met the following week, and Ted felt they had a cordial, productive meeting. He learned that Erik was from a single-parent family and had a very close relationship with the basketball coach, who had been a father figure for him. As the end of his college years loomed, Erik leaned heavily on his coach for mentoring. Ted didn't try to oversell or strong-arm the coach on the merits of his company, but he did have an opportunity to present his organization in the best possible light. Ted felt that a real connection was established.

Toward the end of the meeting Coach Monahan said, "Ted, I've enjoyed getting to know you. Your company sounds as if it would be a very good place to work. I hope you understand that I'm in a mentoring position and I can help Erik to sort through his options, but I cannot put pressure on him nor can I make the decision for him."

Ted responded, "Coach, I absolutely agree. I wouldn't want you to do that. We are looking for people who really want to work in our industry and our company. Frankly, it costs approximately one year's salary to recruit, hire, bring onboard, and train a new employee, and we want people who want to be with us. I just want to thank you for giving me a chance to present the opportunity that we have offered to Erik."

When Erik decided to accept a position with Ted's company, he was ecstatic. It wasn't until a few months later, however, that Ted found out what really happened. Erik had joined the company, and he and Ted were having lunch for the first time. Ted asked how the first few months had gone. Erik told Ted that he was having a great time and he owed it to his basketball coach. He explained that he had made the decision to stick close to home and accept a position with a small company that would be very comfortable for him. When he was reviewing his thought process, the coach asked some questions that led Erik to reconsider his decision. It was these conversations that eventually convinced Erik to reach out and take the riskier, but much higher potential position with Ted's company. Ted recognized that some of the content of those discussions came from his meeting with Coach Monahan.

Strong people skills: empathy, graciousness and the ability to read a social or professional situation

Kumiko was Gwen's sponsor in the interview process, and she was confident that Gwen would do as well in her tenth, eleventh, and twelfth interviews as she had done in the first nine. She knew these interviews represented the last round, and that they were with individuals who would be keys to Gwen's success.

Kumiko greeted Gwen and walked her to the interview with Malcolm. As Kumiko left, she felt a twinge. Gwen seemed a little more quiet and reserved than on previous meetings. The feeling left quickly as Kumiko faced the tasks of the day. An hour later, she headed back to take Gwen to her next interview.

As Gwen and Malcolm finished their conversation, Malcolm asked if he could see Kumiko for a moment. Kumiko asked Gwen to wait for her in reception and she went to see Malcolm. He was blunt and told Kumiko, " You were thorough in giving us the summary of Gwen's background, skills, and abilities and a brief personality sketch. I must tell you that I did not see the person you described. She was shy and quiet, definitely not extroverted and outgoing, as has proven successful in our client service representatives." Kumiko remembered the sensation she had an hour earlier. Her intuition, and Malcolm's comments, told her that something was up.

She thanked Malcolm and went back to Gwen. She sat down and asked if everything was okay. Gwen responded, "Sure, why?" Kumiko told her about her initial feeling and then about Malcolm's comments. As Gwen looked at Kumiko her eyes filled with tears. She explained that her father had died five years ago and last night her mother, who had been feeling ill, was diagnosed with cancer. She had been at the hospital most of the night, checking her in and establishing a game plan with the doctors.

Kumiko didn't hesitate in telling Gwen she was sorry about her mother and that she should be with her. "But I need the job," Gwen protested.

Kumiko responded, " You'll have plenty of time to win a job. I'll retrigger your round of interviews once you get your personal responsibilities under control. Now go and be with your mother." Initially, Gwen didn't want to go, but with Kumiko's gentle insistence, she left to be with her mother. Kumiko did exactly what she said she would. She explained what had happened to Malcolm and he immediately said, "Just forget about today. Have her come back to see me when she is ready." The other interviewers were equally willing to reschedule.

When Gwen came back, she was the person Kumiko described. She exhibited the outgoing, positive personality the earlier interviewers had met. Everyone thought she was great and an offer was made shortly after the interviews. Gwen never forgot the kindness. When she had three excellent offers from outstanding organizations in front of her, she had no difficulty deciding that she wanted to work for Kumiko.

Team oriented: respects others and builds mutual trust; develops partnerships by helping others grow and develop

As Beth interviewed for the position, she knew she would have a close working relationship with Dan, her potential boss. She also knew, from her networking efforts, this firm had a reputation as a difficult place to enter from the outside. This represented a red flag to her.

Beth found herself evaluating Dan's management style every chance she got; in part because his office would be next to hers at headquarters, and he would be her guide. If he were a team player who would mentor her as she learned the job, then she would have a chance to succeed. If he had a sink-or-swim mentality, then she could easily fail.

The critical interaction came during their fourth meeting, when they really got into management style. When Beth asked Dan how he characterized his style, he said, "Beth, I view the relationship we would have as a team venture. You could not be successful here without a lot of help and mentoring in the beginning. You'd have to learn the personalities and how to deal with them internally while learning about the clients and their needs externally. You also know how lean our organization is.

"Consequently, I'd expect you to assimilate information quickly, learn where and how you could add value, and become independent as quickly as possible. Our relationship would then be one of partners. I'd expect you to be productive, and to know when to involve me and to what degree. I need strong business people on my team, not 'yes' people. And I'd expect you to be a strong team player."

Beth liked what Dan had to say, and it seemed to fit with the reference checks she had received. She knew she would have to continue to test what Dan was telling her about his management style with the reality of what it was like to work for him on a day-to-day basis. This could only be done by interviewing with Dan's direct and indirect reports. Fortunately, Dan's company believed in holding numerous interviews before making a decision about a candidate.

By the time Beth had been through the eight required interviews, she had convinced herself that Dan was for real. The interviews gave her an opportunity to test what Dan had told her about his management style with people who reported to him.

His reports gave him high marks. Beth believed that there was an excellent chance she could be successful and find a new home with Dan's company. She accepted Dan's job offer and eagerly joined his team.

Consultative: listens for understanding and problem solving and articulates vision clearly; seeks creative and imaginative solutions

Michael was really struggling with his decision, and it was a momentous one. Harvard Medical School or Johns Hopkins Medical School?

Michael approached the decision in the same technical, analytical manner in which he had approached his engineering studies at Purdue University. It obviously worked well, since he had been awarded one of the highly prestigious Whitaker Fellowships for complete tuition reimbursement at the school of his choice. Michael had selected a career in medical research and, through his own research and discussions with friends, had defined a list of questions upon which to rate the schools.

The list read, in part:
- How much research is done and what kind is it?
- Is the emphasis more academic or on clinical medicine?
- How many endorsements are there for research?
- How much autonomy does the research function have?
- What is the financial stability of the institution?
- How strong is the faculty?
- How closely tied are the hospital and the research facility?
- How international is the medical education and the hospital?

It was a disciplined way to approach his task. It helped Michael screen his list down to his two finalists. However, it no longer helped him to discriminate between those last two enviable choices.

As the decision time drew to the final hours, Michael decided to have one final round of conversations with his proposed professor-mentor in each institution. He called and both professors were out. Michael could do nothing but leave voice mail messages, which he did.

That evening at midnight Michael received a call from the professor at Johns Hopkins. He apologized for the late hour but said that he was in the airport in Chicago, awaiting a continuing flight to a conference where he would be the keynote speaker the next day. The professor and Michael had a productive conversation that lasted for almost an hour and covered a wide range of topics, including the difficulty of Michael's choice. The professor acted primarily as a consultant, helping Michael sift through his thoughts. When the conversation ended, the professor told Michael he hoped he would come to Johns Hopkins and wished him good luck in making his decision.

Michael heard from the Harvard professor the next afternoon. The conversation was shorter than the one the night before, but very congenial. Michael was surprised at his own reaction. He had clearly made the decision to attend Hopkins the night before and now was merely seeking confirmation to justify the decision. The attention the Hopkins professor gave Michael at just the right time was deeply appreciated. It also won Hopkins a prime recruit.

Optimistic: positive, self-confident and persuasive; has enormous energy with the ability to energize and invigorate others

Paige was up to her eyeballs in work, with her international studies semester exams staring her in the face, and her sister's wedding in less than a week. She was needed at home by Thursday night and she wasn't sure she'd be able to pull it off. The final straw was when the airline told her she had called too late, and there were no available seats for Thursday. When she hung up, she was in tears.

Five minutes later, the phone rang. It was Adam, the Director of Recruiting at the firm where she had done her internship last summer. He was calling to wish her well at her sister's wedding.

Paige was dumbstruck; "I can't believe you remembered my sister's wedding."

"When we discussed it last summer, you seemed so excited. How are you managing everything on your plate?"

Paige responded, "Not very well." She then told Adam about her dilemma with the airline and the flight home.

Adam offered, "Let me see if there is anything I can do; sometimes our internal travel agents have pull with the airlines. You understand that you'd have to pay for the trip."

"Of course," Paige answered. "If you could help, I'd be really grateful."

Adam was on the problem the first thing the next morning and within two days, he was able to produce a ticket. Paige was appreciative when Adam called her back. She made it home and had a spectacular time at the wedding. Several months later, when Paige accepted a position at Adam's company and rejected another outstanding offer, she told her new boss that a major factor in helping her decide was the kindness Adam had shown her.

Leadership: remarkable people orientation; intelligent, decisive, known to set and meet aggressive targets; client centered with a passion for excellence

Frank knew the score as he sat in front of the master. Charlie was only a few years from retirement and he had almost become a legend during his working career. He was acknowledged to be one of the most knowledgeable people in the computer industry.

Charlie knew the marketplace better than anyone and was intimately involved with the products, having full knowledge of their strengths and weaknesses. What separated him from the rest, however, was his incredible passion for product excellence and client service. This reputation, built over four decades, enabled Charlie to transact the most complex and profitable business for his firm.

Charlie only accepted two associates a year to work in his group, and Frank was clearly on the way to an offer. He would be the envy of his graduating class at the University of Chicago if he landed this assignment. But Frank knew he wasn't home free yet.

Frank's concern had to do with Charlie's style. Charlie was known to be a tyrant with his associates. He ordered them around as if they were indentured servants and barked and shouted at them like he was an officer dealing with his troops during battle. Frank had learned during his 26 years that that was not the best work style for him. He had learned the hard way that asking for justification or even a "why? " sometimes had dire consequences for him with some professors during his academic experience. Frank knew he sometimes issued the challenge prior to his internal governor stopping him, and that could be a serious problem with this boss.

Charlie couldn't have been more charming during the interview. He clearly had on the sales hat and knew that Frank was a prize catch. Afterwards, Frank did a great deal of due diligence. He spoke with a number of Charlie's former associates. What he discovered corroborated what he had learned previously. Charlie was even more difficult to live with now than he had been some years ago. Frank also learned, however, that in terms of his abilities, Charlie was still as formidable as ever. What Frank could learn would be invaluable for the rest of his career. The "calling card" of having worked for Charlie would be worthwhile in itself.

Frank understood his dilemma. He contacted a former University of Chicago classmate, Vanessa, who was also Charlie's current associate and asked if they could have coffee.

At the critical point in the discussion, Vanessa said to him, "Look, I wasn't comfortable with his style either. I had the background to be able to select a boss whose interpersonal style would be more enjoyable for me. But when I looked at everything he had to offer, I convinced myself that, once in a while, someone is so successful that it's worth the negatives to work for him. Besides, I decided I would give it one or two years and then, if it didn't work out, I would leave, yet still be stronger for the experience.

"To my amazement, he has been much more pleasant than anything I heard. The other associates and I were asking each other the other day whether he has secretly mellowed, or whether we were so well prepared that almost any behavior would seem better than we expected."

Frank thanked Vanessa and as he thought about her comments, he decided it was the right decision for him as well. That meeting, more than any other, helped him decide to accept the offer.

Summary

The impact outstanding interviewers, who also serve as recruiters, have on the hiring process cannot be overemphasized. It is often the major determinant in whether a candidate accepts or rejects an offer.

The characteristics of the best interviewers are:
- Highest character: integrity and maturity.
- Self-awareness: exercises self-control and has knowledge of company strengths and weaknesses.
- Being centered: balanced with strong business ethics and values.
- Strong people skills: empathy, graciousness, and the ability to read a social or professional situation.
- Team oriented: respects others and builds mutual trust; develops partnerships by helping others grow and develop.
- Consultative: listens for understanding and problem solving, and articulates vision clearly; seeks creative and imaginative solutions.
- Optimistic: positive, self-confident, and persuasive; has enormous energy with the ability to energize and invigorate others.
- Leadership: remarkable people orientation; intelligent, decisive, known to set and meet aggressive targets; client-centered with a passion for excellence.

Step 19: Negotiate the Offer

As the interviewing process winds to a successful end, two things should be occurring simultaneously:
- The organization is coming to the conclusion that you are the best fit and offers you a position.
- Your due diligence indicates that the company has all the ingredients that excite, motivate, and challenge you, and provides a forum for you to do your best.

It would be highly unusual to reach this point in a discussion with each side having no prior knowledge of the salary parameters. If you are newly graduated, then the interviewer knows you would be placed at the same point as other new graduates with your education level. If you have experience, it is highly likely that someone, usually a screening recruiter or human resources professional, has discovered what you were making in your last position.

Recent Graduate

If you are a recent graduate or have only a few years of experience, you may not have the luxury of negotiating an offer. If you are negotiating with a mid-size or large company, the human resources professional most likely tells you that the salary for entry level associates is $X and the benefit package is Y.

If it is a smaller company, and you are the only one being hired, you may have a small amount of negotiating leverage. While you have little or no leverage, you can still begin the learning process for future moves. The normal rule of thumb is to try to hold off the salary discussion for as long as possible so your leverage increases.

Interview Tip! Salary Discussion
Try to hold off a discussion of salary for as long as possible.
At a later date, when the company has "fallen in love" with you, you gain additional leverage.

When you sit down to negotiate, you want to talk about what you can do for the company before you ask for fair compensation and benefits. You might say, "Mr. Jones, I'm excited about the possibility of joining your company. I have heard the four major challenges I will face in the first year, and I want you to know that I believe I have the skills to perform effectively and I will work extremely hard to fulfill your expectations."

Always talk about what you can do for the company (achieve its goals) before you talk about what the company can do for you (total compensation package including benefits.)

You will want to ask your potential boss or the human resources executive to explain how the salary structure works, what a typical career progression might be, at what point someone is eligible for the bonus pool, stock options and so on. Many young professionals don't find out about these things because they don't ask.

Attitude is absolutely critical in negotiating an offer. You should approach it from a win-win perspective where you are attempting to work out a package that is fair to the company and good for you. Anything short of this causes you to be unhappy or causes the company to feel you robbed them. The response is then to exact blood from you in return.

You must remain calm, objective, and businesslike. Do your homework before arriving at the negotiation, and have your issues written down so you don't forget them. Remember that when the negotiating is over, you will be working together, and you want it to be on the best possible terms.

Candidate with Experience

As you gain experience (even a few years,) negotiating an offer becomes possible, although within a fairly narrow range. All companies do not pay at the same level, but, when hiring a new employee, most hiring managers like to give an important hire an increase over their previous position. This opens up possibilities for negotiation.

Two important factors for mid-size and large companies are that most positions are covered by two or three different salary ranges and you would like to enter a new position below the 50th percentile of a range because that allows your boss more leeway to give you greater salary increases. If the human resources executive indicates the salary you are discussing is at the high end of the salary range, ask if it is possible to move you to a higher range (so that your salary is lower on the new range and presumably below the 50th percentile for that salary range.)

If your salary is in the midlevel, say $40,000 to $70,000, the approach is the same as in our prior discussion, but you normally have a little more room to negotiate. Let's say that in your previous job your salary was $45,000, there was no bonus, and you had two weeks' vacation and a benefit package. Suppose the interviewer offered you $47,000, no bonus, and two weeks' vacation. You had hoped for a better package. You would thank the interviewer, tell her how excited you are about the potential of working together, and ask for a day or two to think about the offer and to investigate the benefit package.

When you return to negotiate, you have another opportunity to build rapport and to make sure you understand all aspects of the position including the job objectives.

Interview Tip: Focus

Always talk about what you can do for the company (achieve its goals) before you talk about what the company can do for you (total compensation package including benefits.)

Then the conversation might proceed as follows:

Interviewer: Are you prepared to accept our offer?

Candidate: I'm really excited about the potential of working with you. There are just a few issues I'd like to discuss.

Interviewer: What are they?

Candidate: I thought the benefit package was outstanding, but I'd like to talk about the base salary, bonus, and vacation.

Interviewer: Let's take your questions one at a time.

Candidate: I appreciate the offer of a base salary of $47,000. From my recent study of the marketplace, other firms seemed to be paying somewhat higher, and I wondered if you had any flexibility.

Interviewer: What did you have in mind?

Candidate: My study found that $52,000 to $55,000 was closer to market value.

Interviewer: What other issues did you have?

Candidate: I wondered whether this position was bonus-eligible, and whether there was any flexibility in the vacation?

Interviewer: At the current salary, the position is not bonus-eligible and the vacation allocation in this company is strictly according to policy. However, there may be some flexibility and I'm willing to go to bat for you.

Candidate: Thanks so much. I really appreciate that.

As in the previous example, you have taken your one shot at negotiating. When the interviewer comes back with the offer, you either accept it or move on.

Let's assume the interviewer comes back with the following:
Interviewer: I'm happy to tell you that I was able to get you a base of $52,000 and, at that level, there is a maximum 10% bonus possibility. The vacation, however, must remain at two weeks for the first three years.

Your response might be:
> *Candidate*: That's wonderful. I accept and I really appreciate your efforts on my behalf. I will work hard as a member of your team.

Interview Tip! Negotiation
You only get one shot at negotiating an offer. Listen to the total offer, including compensation and non-compensation items, take time to think about the offer, and then, if necessary, come back to negotiate the offer.

Summary

Negotiating the offer is an opportunity for you to demonstrate important professional skills, assist the interviewer to create a win-win agreement that will have everyone feeling good, and continue the bonding process.

Negotiating skills include:
- Preparation for negotiating.
- Professional demeanor that is objective and businesslike.
- The desire to create a win-win agreement.

(Note: Once you have landed your job Appendix C provides you with the unwritten employment contract which spells out how the employer and employee should behave while they are working together.)

Step 20: Cross the Finish Line

Anna knew exactly what she wanted to happen in her interview for a marketing job in a consumer products company. The personal interaction with Carter, the product manager, had been pleasant and their conversation had uncovered a number of mutual friends and common interests. Smiles and a relaxed flow defined the conversation.

When Carter changed the focus to business, he continued in the same relaxed style. When Anna realized she was able to generate business needs, she felt confident. The conversation was a 50-50 percent business discussion from the start. "Perfect—this meeting is going so well," she thought. After generating and clarifying needs, the conversation turned to what the company was doing to solve them. The remainder of the meeting seemed to be a textbook case of how to conduct an interview. When she left, Anna rated herself an A.

When she received the rejection letter two weeks later, she was astounded. She called Carter immediately, but he was not in. She called him every other day for two weeks. Finally, she got him on the telephone at six o'clock one evening. Blunt and honest, she said, "I thought we had a great interview. I couldn't believe the rejection letter."

Surprisingly, Carter was just as blunt, saying, "Look, I really liked you. You have a great background, went to all the right schools, and your prior experience was terrific. But I work in an aggressive, competitive environment, and your style showed me none of that. You developed needs and confirmed them, but you never told me what you were going to do to help me solve them. You'd never survive in this climate as a wallflower. You also never told me you wanted the job or asked me for it. So I didn't give it to you. It was as simple as that."

Anna couldn't believe what she had done. She had followed the process up until the sell and the close. She knew that to achieve the outcome she wanted, she needed to be aggressive and she had not been. She got lulled to sleep and she lost sight of her full agenda.

In addition, she realized she had lost a huge opportunity with someone like Carter, who was a candid and open communicator. If, during the interview, she had asked, "Am I on track?" Carter probably would have given her signals, either verbal or nonverbal, that would have screamed out at her: Anna, you're not here merely to make the interviewing process work as well as the X's and O's on a coach's blackboard. You're here to get a job and I am an aggressive guy, in an aggressive company, in an aggressive industry. Despite the style I am using to conduct the interview, you'd better show some aggressiveness in accomplishing your objectives, and then test to see how you're doing.

But she hadn't, and she had lost. For three days, she licked her wounds. As she replayed the final conversation with Carter in her mind, she remembered he had clearly said he didn't give her the job because she didn't ask for it. However, he didn't say he had hired anyone else. " Maybe," Anna thought, "it's not too late."

She called Carter's secretary and leveled with her about what had happened. Anna asked whether the position had been filled. The answer that came back was "No," but Carter was seeing a lot of people and was very close to a decision.

Anna knew she couldn't wait. She called again around six o'clock. Carter picked up the phone. When he discovered it was Anna he tried to be courteous, but it was clear he wanted to get her off the phone. This time, however, Anna was very clear on her outcome goals. She was extremely precise about how she could help Carter with specific examples of aggressive accomplishments and she completed her sales presentation in about 90 seconds. She told Carter her goal had been 60 seconds and she apologized for the additional 30 seconds. Her agenda was clear: interview me again. He did. She asked for the job, was offered the job, and accepted it.

We're at the end of the journey and you are ready. You've internalized the need for Preparation, Presence, Presentation and Passion. Your preparation has your self-confidence sky high. You are ready for one or multiple interviews, and you have full knowledge of your competencies and accomplishments.

As you look forward to the interview, your goals are crystal clear. You engage the interviewer in a challenging, fun and intellectually stimulating conversation, which demonstrates your presence. Building rapport with the interviewer is of critical importance because this is the basis for determining if you are the best fit for her company.

As the interviewer makes the transition to the business portion of the interview, your presentation skills are in evidence as you concentrate on helping the interviewer accomplish her agenda, which is to determine whether you have the professional skills to be successful in the job. As this goal is accomplished, pockets of opportunity allow you to accomplish your agenda, which is to understand the interviewer's business goals and sell your abilities to accomplish them. Since your behavior is proactive, you demonstrate the initiative and drive that are vital in today's business climate.

Finally, as we saw in the story above, passion for the work, the industry and the company is the great tiebreaker and the reason that you will win the job over a very competitive field. **One last thing, when you find the job you really want, ask for it.** Good luck and God speed.

Appendix A

Key Interview Tips

The interview tips represent a great final review before you interview. The notation indicates where you will find the interview tip in the text.

- Positive thoughts and behavior: You simply cannot allow negative thoughts or comments to infiltrate your presentation. You must be consistently positive in selling your strongest skills and abilities. (The Mind Game)
- Three to Four Competencies: present your three to four best competencies to assist the interviewer to focus on the skill sets you can bring to the organization. (Step 3)
- Value Added Accomplishments: You will be evaluated on the quality of your accomplishments, how they illustrate your ability to achieve the competency and the bottom line contribution. (Step 3)
- The Extra 20-30 Percent: The more you can demonstrate how your skills can help you to do the 20 to 30 percent of the job you haven't done before, the more persuasive you are in the interview. (Step 3)
- Business Accomplishments: Always have more academic and/or business success stories than you will need. (Step 3)
- Physical Exercise: Exercising on the day of the interview enables you to relax and gives you a chance to focus. Exercise 60 to 75 percent of a normal workout. (Step 10)
- Scheduling: Leave plenty of time at both ends of the interview so that you arrive early and can remain late. This reduces stress and shows interest. (Step 10)
- Dress: Your dress should be appropriate and on the conservative side for the company (and industry.) (Step 10)
- Professionalism: Have all pertinent materials and information, such as extra résumés, and company research. Anticipate having to wait before you are interviewed. (Step 10)
- Congenial Attitude: Treat every person you meet as if he were the CEO. He might have a direct connection to the CEO. (Step 10)
- Flexibility: Being flexible is a huge benefit. It allows you to take advantage of a situation, or say or do the right thing, without extra time to prepare. (Step 10)
- Positive Comments: Speak only positively about everyone you know. (Step 11)
- Initial Greeting: A warm smile and a firm handshake make a strong first impression. (Step 11)

- Rapport Building: Do not cut the rapport building short. It is a great opportunity for bonding. The interviewer will transition the interview to a business discussion when she is ready. (Step 11)
- Eye Contact: Make eye contact throughout the interview. This is particularly critical when being asked about potential concerns or weaknesses. (Step 11)
- Timeline: Ask the interviewer about a timeline for filling the position. Knowing that enables you to manage the timing of your job campaign effectively. (Step 11)
- Answering Questions: Answer the interviewer's questions directly and concisely. This gives the interviewer confidence that you are willing to help accomplish her agenda. (Step 12)
- Business Conversation: The goal is to create an exciting, stimulating 50-50 percent business conversation throughout the interview. (Step 12)
- Relax. We're serious. Relax! Approach the interview as an enjoyable opportunity. (Step 13)
- Bond: If the interviewer "falls in love" with you, great things can happen. You may be hired, for example. If rapport is not built, nothing good will happen. (Step 13)
- Build Rapport: Don't cut rapport building short. The interviewer does it soon enough. (Step 13)
- 60 Second Rule: You have 60 seconds to make your point, or you will lose the interviewer. (Step 13)
- Developing Needs: Ask what the interviewer's needs are and confirm that you understand them. (Step 13)
- Consultation: Propose how you can help to solve the needs or how the organization can use your skills. (Step 13)
- Problem Solving: Demonstrate flexibility in your approach to problem solving. You might say, "I would try X, gather data, and evaluate how it worked." (Step 13)
- Overcoming Objections: Resolving a concern gives you a terrific opportunity to clarify something you said, to put forth additional skills, and to extend the interview. (Step 13)
- Ask for the Job: Interviewing is no place for the timid. If you find a job you really want, and if you are qualified and well-prepared enough to get an interview, tell the interviewer you want to work for him. (Step 13)
- Positive Attitude: Interviewers look for positive, "can-do" candidates who are self-starters and eager to accept a challenge. (Step 13)

- Thank You Letter: You have five business days to have a thank you letter on each interviewer's desk or you lose the value of the letter. (Step 16)
- Salary Discussion: Try to hold off a discussion of salary for as long as possible. At a later date, when the company has "fallen in love" with you, you gain additional leverage. (Step 19)
- Focus: Always talk about what you can do for the company (achieve its goals) before you talk about what the company can do for you (total compensation package including benefits.) (Step 19)
- Negotiation: You only get one shot at negotiating an offer. Listen to the total offer, including compensation and non-compensation items, take time to think about the offer, and then, if necessary, come back to negotiate the offer. (Step 19)

Appendix B

Potential Interview Questions

The following represent some potential interview questions. How will you answer each of them, giving bottom line results, wherever appropriate?

- Tell me about yourself.
- Why did you choose the college(s) you attended and your major(s)?
- What extra-curricular activities did you participate in? Why?
- What did you like and not like about each of your jobs (or internships)? Why did you leave?
- What do you consider your strongest competencies?
- What is your greatest accomplishment?
- What makes you unique?
- How would friends describe you?
- What is one of your passions?
- Please assess your strengths and weaknesses.
- When have you been disappointed, and how did you deal with it?
- Please describe your professional objectives.
- What is the largest problem you've faced, and how did you handle it?
- How did you resolve a personal conflict involving other people?
- Is there anything you would have done differently to date?
- How do you see yourself functioning as a member of a team? Can you give me an example?
- What is the most creative thing you have ever done?
- When did you initiate change in an organization? Please give the details.
- Please describe a failure and how you dealt with it.
- Can you give me an example of when you had to persuade a student or co-worker to a different point of view?
- What has been one of the single greatest obstacles or challenges you have faced?
- Is there anything else that you think I should know about you?

Appendix C

The Unwritten Employment Contract

Under today's employment contract, both employer and employee share responsibility for providing the company with necessary skills and abilities, which may change over time. The employer is charged with providing the employee with current, cutting-edge, marketable skills. The employee has the responsibility to manage his/her own career.

Company's Responsibility
- Creation of an employment contract that respects the employee and the employer.
- Establishment of a culture where everyone understands the company must continue to provide outstanding goods and services to remain in business.
- Meaningful work with an opportunity to contribute.
- Management that truly cares about their employees.
- Opportunity for career growth and renewal.
- Environment that focuses on constantly renewing employees, rather than using and then harvesting them.

Employee's Responsibility
- Provision of enhanced productivity in meaningful work.
- Commitment to the company's success for the duration of tenure.
- Continuous learning.
- Awareness of one's skills, strengths and weaknesses, and a plan to correct weaknesses.
- Reinvention of oneself, if necessary, to keep pace with change.
- Development of marketable, competitive skills is a joint responsibility of company and employee.
- Management of one's own career.

About the Authors

Frederick W. Ball is Managing Director of Ball & Associates, LLC a human resources consulting firm specializing in career planning/transition and executive coaching. He consults with senior executives and high potential professionals from some of the top companies in the Fortune 500 and the not-for-profit, and education industries. He is a former executive director of the Institute for Administrative Research at Columbia University where he earned his doctorate.

Barbara B. Ball is Director of Human Resources for the prestigious West-field, NJ public schools. Her responsibilities include recruiting and hiring, employee and labor relations, as well as training and development. She has served as Managing Director of Ball & Associates, LLC where she specialized in communications/human resources consulting to Fortune 100 companies, not-for-profit, and education organizations. She is a graduate of Rosemont College (BA) and Kean University (MA).

In addition to their work with senior-level executives at major companies in a range of industries, Fred and Barbara's work also includes over 15 years of delivering seminars and counseling to students at Brown, Columbia, and Duke Universities and other universities on how to land that all-important first job. In group and one-on-one sessions, students learned the skills that gave them the "edge" to nail the job interview and win the most desirable jobs. This experience led Fred and Barbara to establish The Killer Interview Solution, (www.thekillerinterviewsolution.com) a training and coaching practice for students and young professionals, and the basis for this book.

Fred and Barbara are also the co-authors of the highly respected *Killer Interviews: The Best Interview Strategies* (Revised-2010), one of the top resources for executives and rising stars who want to "win" their ideal job, and *Impact Hiring: The Secrets of Hiring a Superstar* (2000), which coaches senior management in the art/skill of hiring top talent. They have guest lectured at Brown University and are nationally known resources to the media appearing on local and national television (NBC, CNN, Fox), radio (WCBS, Source Report), magazines (Parade) and newspapers (New York Times, Chicago Tribune).

www.thekillerinterviewsolution.com

Index

LaVergne, TN USA
22 July 2010
190518LV00007B/196/P